M. Taylor

bandana
t-shirt
flip-flops
jeans
sarong

HEINEMANN PLAYS

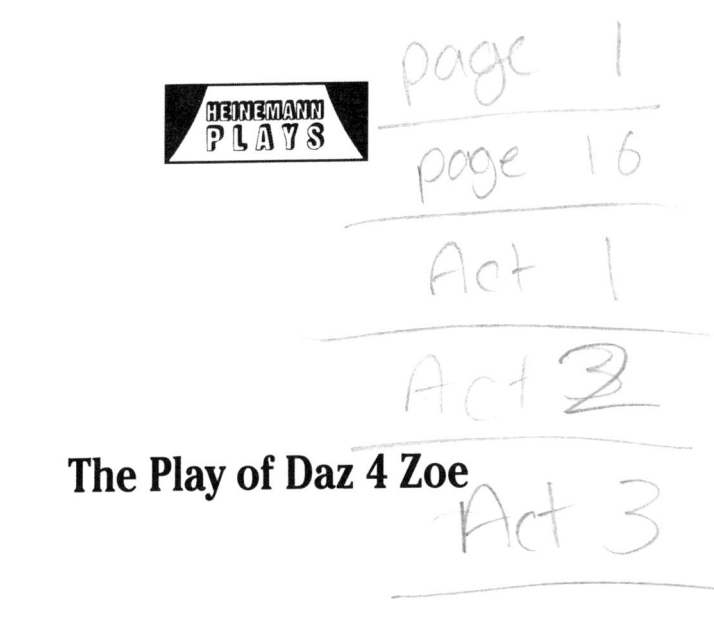

The Play of Daz 4 Zoe

Joe Standerline
Inspired by the novel by Robert Swindells

Introduction by Robert Swindells

Heinemann

Heinemann Educational Publishers
Halley Court, Jordan Hill, Oxford OX2 8EJ
A division of Reed Educational and Professional Publishing Ltd

OXFORD MELBOURNE AUCKLAND
JOHANNESBURG BLANTYRE GABORONE
IBADAN PORTSMOUTH NH (USA) CHICAGO

Play copyright ©2000 Joe Standerline and Robert Swindells
General introduction and Activities ©2000 Joe Standerline

All rights reserved. No part of this publication may be reproduced in any material form (including photocopying or storing it in any medium by electronic means and whether or not transiently or incidentally to some other use of this publication) without the prior written permission of the copyright owner, except in accordance with the provisions of the Copyright, Designs and Patents Act 1988 or under the terms of a licence issued by the Copyright Licensing Agency Ltd, 90 Tottenham Court Road, London W1P 0LP. Applications for the copyright owner's written permission to reproduce any part of this publication should be addressed in the first instance to the publisher.

04 03 02 01 00
10 9 8 7 6 5 4 3 2 1

ISBN 0 435 23329 7

Cover design by The Point
Cover illustration by Barry Patterson
Typeset by Tek-Art, Croydon, Surrey
Printed and bound in the United Kingdom by Clays Ltd, St Ives plc

CAUTION
All rights whatsoever in these plays are strictly reserved and on no account may performances be given unless written permission has been obtained before rehearsals commence from Heinemann Educational Publishers.

CONTENTS

Introduction by Robert Swindells	iv
General Introduction	vi
List of Characters	viii
Setting	xi
Glossary	xii
The Play of Daz 4 Zoe	
Act One	1
Act Two	37
Act Three	85
Before you Read	118
Questions and Explorations	
Keeping Track	119
Act One	119
Act Two	122
Act Three	126
Explorations	130

INTRODUCTION BY ROBERT SWINDELLS

Daz 4 Zoe is a love story which sets out to show what can happen when we don't love enough: when we adopt the poisonous ideas of those who would divide us and permit greed, ignorance and fear to stunt the capacity we're all born with for loving one another.

I have peopled my divided society with privileged Subbies and dispossessed Chippies. This is in the tradition of a bigotry which seeks to diminish groups within society by inviting us to think of them as Beasts, Pansies, Whingers, Scroungers, Losers and so on: it's easier to mistreat people if we can manage to think of them as not fully human.

Daz 4 Zoe is set in the future, or rather it is set in *a* future: a dismal future we're currently drifting towards but might avoid through the power of love. *All you need is love*, sang the Beatles, and that's exactly right. Love unites, everything else divides. Subbies don't love Chippies: they think the Chippies are after what they've got, and they're right. Chippies don't love Subbies: the Subbies have grabbed everything and there's nothing left for the Chippies. There'd be enough for everyone if it was shared out fairly, but first there'd have to be love, and love has been all but swamped by hatred, fear and suspicion.

Note that *all but*, because you can't kill love. Not entirely. Not quite, though it's often been tried. That's why a miracle called Band Aid happened some years ago in spite of a political leader's pronouncement that there is no such thing as society. It happened because people found they cared after all: that there *is* such a thing as society and it extends to wherever there are people – especially people in need. That was love in action. So is Children in Need, attracting millions of pounds in donations year after year. If writing out a modest cheque while wearing a silly red nose isn't *love*, what is it?

Daz loves Zoe, even though she's a Subby. Zoe loves Daz the Chippy, so something's gone wrong with the system. It's not allowed, this love. It's against the law. And *why* is it against the law? Because it's dangerous, that's why. If Subbies and Chippies start loving one another, where's it going to end? They'll be going around together, getting to know each other. Getting to *like* each other, even. Going in each other's houses. Drinking together. Laughing together. Then before you know it two of 'em'll get together and make a baby, and what will it *be*, this baby? A Subby? A Chippy? A *Chubby*? You can see it's dangerous. The whole set-up starts unravelling. No, it's got to be stopped. Stopped before it starts.

But *how*, if you can't kill love . . .

Bob Swindells

GENERAL INTRODUCTION

On first reading *Daz 4 Zoe* I felt ill at ease. It left me with feelings of sadness, even anger, but I didn't quite know why. I was drawn to the love story between Daz and Zoe, but I found it difficult to understand how some of the other characters could behave in the ways they did.

Robert Swindells had created a terrible world and let me experience the violent and desperate behaviour of its people. I had been introduced to a society that I would never want to visit. It was then I realised – this imaginary world is not so different from my own. Stories like this one happen to real people. Perhaps this was the source of my anger: I was reacting to very real situations, not just a series of ideas or events imagined by an author.

In the novel, Daz and Zoe speak directly to the reader and, for much of the time, they are isolated from each other and from most of the people they would normally turn to. When writing a play, the usual rule is to show events taking place, rather than simply to have your characters talk about them. I didn't want to use long and potentially complicated monologues and so had to find a different way of telling their story. In doing so, numerous locations and characters are used. If you don't read plays that often, it might help to look at the suggestions on page 118 before you start.

This play might make you feel uncomfortable, even angry in places. In a sense, I hope it does. This story is too close to real life to be squashed into a nicely resolved package. I was tempted to try at times. I love a happy ending as much as the next person but, deep down, I knew this would be inappropriate. A happy ending is not necessarily a positive one.

A love story such as this deserves a more truthful telling. As Daz himself says towards the end of the play: *'It's not a fairy story'*.

Joe Standerline

LIST OF CHARACTERS

The Subbies

Gran	Great-grandma to Zoe. Sprightly. Wise. Optimistic.
Zoe Askew	Aged 14. Bright. Impetuous. Free-spirited.
Gerald Askew	Zoe's father. Bigoted. Scared of what people think of him.
Amanda Askew	Zoe's mother. Passive. Non-threatening. Likes to clean things.
Larry Turner	Aged 14. Acquaintance of Tabitha's. Loud. Arrogant. Irritating.
Tabitha Wentworth	Aged 14. Called Tab. Zoe's best friend. Rich. Fun. Mature.
Ned Volstead	Aged 15. Tim's friend. Intelligent. Adventurous.
Tim Bixby	Aged 14. Ned's friend. Generous. Under-confident.
Mrs Moncrieff	Teacher. Stressed. Blinkered. Strict.
Mr James	Teacher in Chippy school. Honourable. A caring Subby.
Paul Wentworth	Tabitha's father. Wealthy. Resourceful. Good-natured.
Mrs Wentworth	Tabitha's mother.

The Chippies

Cal	Leader of DRED organisation. Dedicated. Reserved. Calculating.
Jay	DRED member.
Dave Lawson	DRED member. School caretaker. Close friend of Zena's.
Nel	DRED member. Passionate. Strong. Committed.

List of Characters

Trev	New DRED member. Eager to learn.
Mick	Aged 17. DRED member. Cal's 'yes man'. Knows Daz. Disloyal.
Abbo	Member of DRED. Loyal.
Mrs Barraclough	Daz's mother. Suffers from depression. Kind heart.
Darren Barraclough	Known as Daz. Brave. Bright. Noble. Trusting.
Zena Metcalf	FAIR member. Lawson's friend. Maid for Wentworths. Dedicated.
Bouncer	Works in Blue Moon Club. Hard. Good sense of humour.
Shaker	DRED member. Barman in Blue Moon Club.
Roz	Daz's ex-girlfriend. Bitter. Hard.
Mel	Quiet. Client in Blue Moon Club.
Jim	Mel's boyfriend. Hard. Aggressive. Threatening.
Macka	Jim's sidekick.
Johnson	DRED member.
Cooper	DRED member.
Taylor	Goes to school with Daz.
Alex	Goes to school with Daz.
Dawn	Goes to school with Daz.
Martha	Cleaning lady. Saucy. Enjoys a laugh.
Connie	Cleaning lady. Saucy. Tries to adopt airs and graces.
Alf	Street kid.
Sue	Street kid.
John	Street kid.

Domestic Services

Lieutenant Pohlman	Enjoys his job. Twisted. Malicious. Prone to violence.
Sergeant Dawes	Works for Pohlman. Surprisingly kind.
Officer Adams	Professional. Does as he is told.
Officer Blake	Professional. Does as he is told.

Officer Linden	A no-nonsense sort of woman.
Officer Mian	Professional. Does as he is told.

Youthopia Team

Nigel	TV presenter. False. Shallow. Patronising.
Norma	TV presenter. False. Shallow. Patronising.
Felicity McColgan	TV news reporter. Ambitious. Callous. 'Nice' in front of a camera.
Pippa	Aged 15. Well-spoken Subby.
Edward	Aged 15. Well-spoken Subby.
Doctor	Typical 'TV doctor'.

The School Play

Played by Zoe's classmates:

Narrator	Without character.
Savage One	Caricature of a Chippy.
Savage Two	Caricature of a Chippy.
Savage Three	Caricature of a Chippy.
Landowner	Played as an innocent victim.
Leader	Caricature of Cal.
Sampson	Caricature of the 'Sampson' figure.

Non-Speaking Roles

Kids in Subby school scenes.
Kids in Chippy school scenes.
Chippies in border gate scenes.
Clients in Blue Moon Club.
Clients in Black Diamond Bar.
Staff at Silverdale Medical Facility.

SETTING

The Play of Daz 4 Zoe is set in the late twenty-first century. Society has been divided into two sections, the 'haves' and the 'have nots'. The less privileged Chippies are forced to live in Inner City slums, separated from their wealthy neighbours by a heavily guarded border. The others, the Subbies, live in luxurious suburbs and most choose to ignore the inequality and oppression of which they are a part. Some Inner City dwellers are employed to work in the suburbs but their wages are poor, they have little or no rights and they are forced to return home to their ghetto before dark. The only time a Subby would move to the Inner City would be if they had been banished there. A few are allowed in for the purposes of work but for the rest of the Subbies, crossing the border is forbidden. Of course, not everyone lives by the rules.

GLOSSARY

Language

Blue stuff	(Chippy slang) Water.
Brain-Drain	An alcoholic cocktail.
Chippies	People who live in the Inner City.
Chippyville	The Inner City.
Deletion	Subby term for an execution (humane deletion).
DRED	A group of freedom fighters (led by Cal).
Doodies	(Chippy slang) Clothes.
DS	Domestic Security (formerly the police force).
Dulleye	(Chippy slang) A form of clinical depression.
FAIR	Name of a pacifist organisation (led by Sampson).
Kick-out	(Chippy slang) A Subby banished to the Inner City.
Lobotomiser	Another alcoholic cocktail.
Peanuts	Money.
Shooter	Gun.
Subbies	People who live in the suburbs.

Stage Directions

(beat)	A short pause.
(VO)	Voice over.
(off)	Voices heard from offstage.

For my mum, Diane Laynes

ACT ONE

Scene One

It is Friday the 11th. A sterile beam of light shines down on Gran. She is in a small, plain space with only a chair. She's doing an aerobic routine.

Gran So many dreams, so many mountains. Seventy-four years ago, I became somebody's mother, forty after that, I started being a grandma. (*Hand on heart*) I'm as young as I ever was in here, though. (*Starts to twist from side to side*) Just as young, and maybe just as foolish. Our Zoe thinks I should have myself done. 'All your friends have . . .' she says, '. . . Mrs Wentworth looks younger than her daughter these days, Gran . . . You don't act like a hundred and four years old, why should you have to look like it?' 'Easy,' I said, 'That's what I am!' (*Stands still, regains her breath*) I'm her *great*-grandma really. She prefers 'Gran'. She probably thinks *I* prefer it. (*Pause*) You'd think things would slow down as you get older but they don't. Life hurtles on. (*Sits down*) Look at this place. Fifty years ago, this was *the* place to live. Everyone wanted to move here. Because of that, the house prices went (*beat*) . . . I was going to say 'through the roof', but you know what I mean. Before too long, only the wealthy newcomers could afford to buy one. Those that had grown up here had to make other arrangements. In fifty years we've gone from the most desirable area in the country to a

1

. . . to a mess, basically. Now we're left with a few people having too much and far too many without enough. I saw it coming, we all did. There are two groups of people who believe they can do something about all this. DRED are the violent ones. Don't ask me what it means. I think it's designed to frighten people. 'Freedom Fighters', they call themselves. I call it terrorism. Violence is violence. The others are known as FAIR: 'The Fraternal Alliance for Integration through Reunification'. You can call yourself what you like, actions always speak louder than words. (*Still sitting, she starts to touch her toes.*) And there's the DS of course, they're responsible for keeping us all in our place. They used to be the police force. Someone, somewhere must have thought 'Domestic Security' sounds better. (*Stops*) 'So many mountains.' I've climbed my share, don't worry. The trouble is, the few that are left have got a whole lot bigger recently.

We hear a loud, echoing 'clunk'. Gran's little room is plunged into darkness.

Scene Two

Nine days earlier. Afternoon of Wednesday the 2nd. DRED HQ. The location is underground, it looks cold and damp. DRED members are gathered, joking and sparring with one another. One stands near the front, holding a tray with a glass and a small jug of water. Cal enters. He stands behind a lectern at the front of the meeting place. Everyone falls silent.

Act One, Scene Two

Cal That's more like it. As some of you know, our recent effort to procure arms has been thwarted. The weapons did not arrive at the designated drop-off point, which leaves us in a very unfortunate position . . .

Jay Was it the dealers, Cal, have they ripped us off?

Cal (*ignores her*) The operation was sabotaged.

Lawson Sampson's doing?

Nel (*to a colleague*) No one else would dare.

Cal (*to Nel*) You have something to say, Nel?

Nel No, Cal.

Cal Sampson has claimed responsibility. Once again, the FAIR movement has interfered with the course of justice. Many of our members remain imprisoned, and no doubt many more will be before we resolve this situation. The FAIR organisation now has over three hundred automatic weapons at its disposal. This gives me grave cause for concern.

Jay But they're pacifists, Cal. Sampson would never let his members use guns, it's . . .

Cal Pacifism is a luxury, even to Sampson. We all have our limit. I've drawn up a strategy. No one is to rest until we discover the location of this missing shipment and those responsible are identified and dealt with.

Trev Does this mean the siege is off, then?

Mick Idiot.

Cal The prisoners will be liberated. We simply need more time. Some of you will be going undercover for the investigation. Nel, Abbo? You're to head the suburban campaign, report back to Mick here.

Abbo OK, Cal.

Nel	Right.
Jay	What's the point?
Cal	You have a problem?
Jay	You know I could do this, Cal.
Cal	I don't want you . . .
Jay	I've been trained just as well as these . . .
Cal	The decision has been made. Pay attention. The code name is Ferret. Discussion should be kept to a minimum. The following strategy is to be memorised . . .
Lawson	I think we should keep this on a 'need to know' basis, Cal. It looks like we have a leak somewhere.
Cal	We're all fighting the same cause, Lawson, everyone has the right to know what's happening.
Lawson	But there could still be . . .

Cal takes a revolver from an inside pocket and places it on the lectern.

Cal	I'm sure everyone realises the price of betrayal. (*To Nel*) The Alliance between DRED and FAIR was both short-lived and ill-fated. We do not and cannot accept their whimsical ideals of a peaceful resolution. Sampson has gone too far. Our cause is the quest for a free and just society. Their actions reveal little more than shallow pity and a pathetic need to ease their collective conscience. The FAIR organisation is as much a part of our oppression as those it claims to be opposing. It is time they were disbanded.

The crowd applaud and cheer.

Trev	(*applauding*) What was that about?
Abbo	(*applauding*) Dunno.
Nel	He means we're gonna kick Sampson's ar . . .
Cal	(*shouting*) There's no time for this.

Jay Make me a part of it, Cal. I've been a member for nearly twelve months now. I can make a difference, I want the chance to serve . . .

Cal stares at Jay, she falls silent.

Cal Very well. (*Looks at the person with tray and turns back to Jay*) You can pour.

Reluctantly, Jay fills the glass with water and hands it to Cal.

Trev How do you know it was Sampson, Cal? Has he been in touch or something?

Cal That information is classified.

Lawson So much for the right to know.

Cal (*picking up the gun*) What is this, Lawson?

Lawson It's a revolver, Cal.

Cal And what is it used for?

Mick Taking people out, eh boys?

Cal Shut it, Mick. I asked you a question, Lawson. What do you think this is for?

Lawson Killing.

Cal Jay. What about you?

Jay The same, I suppose.

Cal In the wrong hands, yes. But when used with integrity it offers something far more valuable. (*Aims the gun at Jay*) I call it protection.

Cal fires. Blackout.

Scene Three

Wednesday the 2nd. Late afternoon. On screen, Nigel and Norma sit behind a desk as cheap 'news programme' music is heard. On stage, lights fade up until we can just make out three figures on a sofa. We are in the Askew living room with Zoe, Gerald and Amanda watching TV. Blue light flickers across their faces as they watch.

Nigel Welcome back.

Norma You're tuned to channel 2253 digital, 708 community satellite or www dot slash, Domestic Service Broadcasting, slash *Youthopia* squiggle-dot Free TV. Nigel?

Nigel Thanks, Norma. It doesn't take a genius to know that those living on the other side of the so-called 'Order Border' do not have the same moral fibre as, say, you or I . . .

Norma But is that an excuse to join violent gangs and go around behaving like terrorists?

Nigel And is that the case with all of the Inner City dwellers? Our roving reporter Felicity McColgan is at the border now. Felicity, I believe you've met two very special people?

Cut to a heavily armoured Felicity holding a microphone. She's standing at the border gate.

Felicity That's right, Nige. Behind me you see the famous gate used to let so many of the Inner City dwellers into our suburbs to work. How many of us have stood here as children jeering at the so-called 'Chippy' people, and even thrown the occasional stone? But have we been misjudging them? I'm joined by two young people who are hoping to find out for themselves.

Pippa and Edward come into view.

. . . Pippa and Edward, welcome to *Youthopia*.

Pippa and Edward } Thanks.

Act One, Scene Three

Felicity You're both from the Wentworth housing estate, here on the open side.

Edward That's right.

Felicity (*to camera*) Tonight, with their parents' permission and special security clearance from our friends at Domestic Security, Pippa and Edward are going to spend an entire evening with an Inner City family. (*To Pippa*) So what made you come up with this brave attempt?

Pippa We believe that deep down all people are equal, Felicity. Just because you're poor and uneducated doesn't mean that you're not a good person.

Felicity Really?

Edward OK, some of them are criminals but if you actually try to get to know them, you'll probably find they're quite similar to us.

Felicity You are planning to spend a whole evening on the other side of the border. What do your parents think?

Edward They were really cool, they said it was fine so long as we didn't get too familiar.

Pippa Or let any of them touch us.

Felicity There's a feeling of excitement here tonight but it has to be asked, will this crazy scheme actually help anyone?

Cut back to the studio.

Nigel More from Felicity later.

Norma Taking a risk there, wouldn't you say, Nige?

Nigel It's a free community, Norma.

Norma Join us after the break for another of our popular Career profiles . . .

Nigel Is being a Community Executioner as respectable as they try to tell us?

Both   Be right back.

Music plays once more.

Lights full up on the Askew living room. Gerald switches off the TV. Amanda is flicking through a magazine.

Zoe   Disgusting.

Gerald   They won't last five minutes.

Zoe   As if anyone'd want to kill people for a living.

Gerald   That's not so bad.

Zoe   Except you obviously.

Gerald   Someone's got to do these things.

Zoe   It doesn't mean someone should want to, though.

Gerald   They're savages, Zoe. They have to be shown. Better for them, better for us. You'd soon change your tune if we let them do as they wanted.

Zoe   Pass me an application form. (*Superhero voice*) Zoe Askew: Community Executioner, at your service.

Gerald   Don't start.

Zoe   What's that, madam, your gardener looked at you in a funny way? No fear . . .

Gerald   This isn't funny.

Zoe   . . . I will deal with him. That's nothing a nice little slaughtering session won't fix.

Gerald   The term is 'humane deletion'.

Zoe   (*her usual voice*) You can call it what you like, it's still killing people.

Gerald   There's a difference.

Zoe   How?

Gerald   Don't feel it for one thing.

Zoe   Bet their families do.

Act One, Scene Three

Gerald You'll realise how lucky you are one of these days.

Zoe Once I've grown up, is that it?

Gerald There's plenty would take your place.

Amanda (*still flicking through her magazine*) Politics, politics.

Zoe Mum?

Amanda (*without looking up*) Yes dear?

Zoe What's your favourite way of murdering Chippies?

Gerald (*to Zoe*) You'll be branded a Sympathiser if you're not careful.

Amanda She's only joking.

Gerald People have been killed for less.

Zoe Humanely deleted, surely, Dad?

Gerald (*to Amanda*) This is your grandmother's fault.

Zoe gets up and grabs her bag.

Gerald Where do you think you're going?

Zoe I'm going to turn myself in. It's been nice knowing you both.

Exit Zoe.

Amanda Don't be angry, Gerald.

Gerald There was a time when children respected their parents. If I'd spoken to my father like that he'd have sent me to a boot camp.

Amanda She's rebelling. It's her age, Gerald. We've all done it.

Gerald Speak for yourself.

Scene Four

DRED HQ. The same meeting as before. Cal is drinking his water. Jay's body is on the ground where she fell.

Lawson The last time anyone saw Sampson was thirty or so years ago. Where are we supposed to start?

Cal At the beginning, Lawson.

Abbo If we do find him, Cal, what are we gonna do with him?

Cal I'll leave that to the DS, I think they'll make a better job of it.

Lawson Is that such a good idea? Sampson might have things on us. Handing him over could prove fatal.

Cal Are you doubting my methods, Lawson?

Lawson I'm suggesting you might be letting your anger get the better of you.

Cal I'm in control.

Lawson (*pointing to Jay's body*) Try telling her that.

Cal She was DS.

Lawson Jay?

Cal Protection. As I said.

Nel She knew about the siege plans, Cal . . .

Cal She thought she did. Mick had been feeding her misinformation. Now our plans have been disrupted, she was no longer useful to us. Any further questions?

No reply.

Dismissed. Cooper, Johnson, dispose of this please.

Act One, Scene Five

Two members carry Jay's body away. Mick approaches Cal.

... *(to Mick)* I want you to keep an eye on Lawson for me.

Mick What for?

Cal Something in my water, let's say.

Mick You think he spiked it, Cal?

Cal Just watch him.

Lights down.

Scene Five

Early evening of Wednesday the 2nd. The Barraclough apartment. Daz's mum sits in a battered old rocking chair. Everything looks dirty.

Mrs Barraclough Don't you never go off wiv no DRED. You hear me, Del?

Enter Daz with a pill in his hand.

Daz I'm Daz, Mam.

Mrs Barraclough They's a bad lot them. End up killed. Where's your little brother?

Daz It's time for your medicine. Can you do it without a drink this time?

Mrs Barraclough You can't make me.

Daz Come on, just get it down. Wanna feel happy, don't yer? *(Puts the pill into his mum's mouth)* Make things nice and clear again. Swalla, Mam.

Mrs Barraclough I'm too dry, Daz.

Daz Just have a go.

Mrs Barraclough tries and after a while manages to swallow the pill.

. . . Has it gone?

Mrs Barraclough nods.

. . . Not so bad, was it? You'll be back to your old self in a minute or two. I tell you, one day we'll have that much of the blue stuff you'll be able to soak yourself in it.

Mrs Barraclough Careful I don't drown, eh, Daz?

Daz That's right, Mam. You'll have to take swimming lessons.

Enter Mick, fastening his trousers.

Mick The bucket's full, Daz.

Daz I'll sort it after.

Mick Is she all right?

Daz Will be in a minute.

Mick My old man's got dulleye, not as bad as her though.

Daz Am I in with a chance then?

Mick looks at Mrs Barraclough carefully.

. . . She's not listening, Mick.

Mick I spoke to Cal this afternoon. He'll see you in the Blue Moon on Friday.

Daz Will I have to do anything?

Mick Just be there. He'll probably ask why you want to join up.

Daz Why does anyone? Killin' Subbies.

Mick You are fifteen, aren't yer?

Daz Yeah. Three month ago. He's got to let me in, Mick. Our Del would've wanted me in. I'll be just as good as he was.

Mick Save it for Cal, mate.

Act One, Scene Five

Mrs Barraclough No DRED, you hear, don't you ever go off wiv no DRED . . .

Mick Thought you said . . .

Daz Just the dulleye talkin'. She thinks I'm our Del most the time.

Mick You still miss him then?

Daz What do you think? He was her son same as me. Best brother you could ask for, Del was. I still talk to him sometimes, can't get much out of our Mam these days. Roz thought I was mental.

Mick She still around?

Daz Chucked.

Mick Not putting out, was she?

Daz Not to me, no.

Mick I've gotta shoot, something big's going down. Make sure you're there on Friday.

Daz What's happening?

Mick Can't say, mate.

Daz Come on, Mick.

Mick It's an arms shipment.

Daz Yeah?

Mick They were supposed to arrive at the end of last week. Looks like FAIR got there first. When the crates arrived, they were full of yellow roses. Cal's not a happy man right now.

Daz I'm not surprised. What were they for?

Mick We were gonna storm the DS. It'll have to wait now. Not a word to anyone about this, OK mate?

Daz No problem. What time Friday?

Mick Eight.

Exit Mick.

Mrs Barraclough	Nowt good never come o' killing folk, you hear me, Del?
Daz	It's Daz, Mam. Del's not here.
Mrs Barraclough	Where's our Del?
Daz	Gone to a better place, Mam.

Scene Six

Wednesday the 2nd. Early evening. The Wentworth house. Tabitha's bedroom. Tab is with Ned, Tim, Larry and Zoe. Larry is looking through Tab's music collection.

Larry	Classical rave! (*Reading a sleeve*) ' . . . A soothing collection from the late twentieth century. Lovingly remastered for today's omni-directional listeners . . .'
Tab	Can we get on with it, please?
	Tim picks a different record up.
Larry	Who's Robbie Williams?
Ned	Do you want to do this or not, Turner?
Larry	Here, aren't I?
Ned	I've got my dad's car for the weekend. I suggest we make it this Friday. It'll give us until Monday to recover.
Zoe	(*to Tab*) Recover from what?
Tab	It's OK, Zoe.
Larry	She's terrified already.
Zoe	'She' has got a name.
Tim	You tell him, Zoe.

Act One, Scene Six

Larry flashes a threatening look at Tim.

Tab Zoe's been left out of this for long enough. If you don't like it, Larry, you can make your own arrangements. I've heard the security codes have been changed, we might not be able to get through this time.

Ned Not a problem. (*Produces a small book*)

Zoe (*to Tim*) What's that?

Tim Security codes. His dad's in the DS.

Zoe is shocked, though tries hard not to show it.

Ned We just turn up at the barrier, key in the new codes and head straight for Chippyville.

Zoe Can I ask a question?

Tab Sure.

Zoe How do you get past the guards?

Larry Somebody shoot me!

Tim We go through the DS barrier. It's automated, Zoe.

Zoe Won't there be cameras?

Ned My father works for the Domestic Services, right?

Zoe Right.

Ned From time to time, he has to use his own car to cross the border.

Zoe Yeah?

Larry For Pete's sake! Every DS car has a transponder. (*Patronising*) A transponder is a tiny electronic device which sends and receives signals . . .

Zoe I know what a transponder is.

Ned That's how we get through undetected. The system thinks it's an official entry.

Zoe Have you got to get out of the car to put the code in?

Larry I don't believe this.

Tim He just has to lean out of the window, Zoe.

Ned (*producing an official-looking DS hat*) With this on for good measure.

Tab Is Friday agreed with everyone?

Tim I'm in!

Larry I've nothing better to do. I'm dressing up this time. Show the slum-scum what real 'doodies' look like.

Tab You're a pig, Turner, you know that? They can't help being scruffy . . .

Larry Yeah, same as I can't help being the best-dressed sex-god in Silverdale.

Tab Please?!

Ned You'll stick out like a sore thumb if you do that.

Larry I haven't spent a fortune on new gear to look like a sodding Chippy, have I?

Knock at the door.

Zena (*off*) Miss Wentworth?

Room falls silent.

Tab Come in, Zena.

Zena (*enters*) Your father sent me up. (*To the others*) I'm afraid I'll have to ask you to leave.

Larry I'm sorry?

Zena Miss Wentworth and Miss Askew are supposed to be doing their school work this evening . . .

Larry And you see that as an excuse to throw us all out? Do you want to keep your job?

Zena Sorry, sir?

Tab It's OK, Zena. They were about to make a move anyway.

Zena Thank you, miss.

Act One, Scene Six 17

Exit Zena.

Tab *(to Larry)* There was no need for that.

Larry She's a Chippy maid.

Tab She's *our* Chippy maid, Larry, and she happens to be very nice.

Larry Anyone would think she was DS the way you speak to her.

Tab Grow up, Turner.

Ned *(getting up)* Make sure you get plenty of cash together.

Larry Gonna get the Chippy to let us out then, or you too scared to ask?

Tab Tell you what, Larry. Why don't I ask Ned to let you out? It's all right, he knows the way.

Ned See you Friday, Tab.

Tab Yeah.

Exit Larry and Ned.

Tim I'll stick around for a while if you like.

Tab We've got work to do, Tim.

Tim I don't mind helping, what is it?

Tab We're working on an old phone system. A technology project.

Tim I'm good at technology.

Tab So are we, Tim.

Tab goes to get the phones she and Zoe are working on.

Tim *(to Zoe)* I live near your grandma.

Zoe What?

Tim I see you calling for her sometimes. I'm in the yellow house across the green.

Zoe I thought you lived around here?

Tim Used to. My mum said it was too close to the

border and it only had two garages. Are you sure I can't help with anything?

Tab rejoins them. She has the two mobile phones.

Tab Tim, my dad's pretty strict when it comes to school work.

Tim Sorry, Tab. (*Sees the old phones*) Wow, they're ancient. You'll never get them to work, surely?

Tim whistles and stands there looking at Zoe.

Tab . . . Tim?

Tim Hmm?

Tab Goodbye?

Tim Oh. Sorry, yeah. See you, Zoe.

Zoe (*not looking at him*) Bye.

Exit Tim.

Tab You've got yourself an admirer there.

Zoe Tim?

Tab You could do worse.

Zoe Not much.

Tab You can sit next to him in the car if you like.

Zoe I can't believe you've talked me into this.

Tab It's about time you lived a bit.

Zoe (*spots Ned's code book and picks it up*) He's left his book. Maybe we should go after him.

Tab It'll be all right. He won't need it until Friday.

Zoe How many times have you been?

Tab Six or seven. Stop worrying, Zoe.

Zoe (*leafing through the book*) It's even got the communication codes. Tab, this is so illegal.

Tab Are we doing this or not?

Zoe Sorry. Are they holding their charge now?

Tab One's better than the other. Did you get the video kits?

Act One, Scene Six

Zoe I nearly forgot. (*Takes two small boxes from her bag*) They should work, the woman said. We just need to hardwire an interface.

Tab Did you ask her about supporting the network?

Zoe Anything within fifty years should be fine, it was analogue before that.

They start to work on the phones.

Tab My dad said these were used by Sympathisers.

Zoe How does he know that?

Tab looks uncomfortable suddenly.

Tab (*lying*) The man he bought them from told him. He, erm, tried to make out they were seized when the Inner City got encrypted. He was probably lying to put the price up.

Zoe They don't let the Chippies have anything, do they? Fancy not being able to have phones. I couldn't do without mine.

Tab We could take them with us on Friday.

Zoe (*sarcastic*) They'll be a lot of use over there.

Tab They *would* actually.

Zoe's not with her.

 . . . We've got the codes, remember?

Zoe Of course. They'd work over the border.

Tab It'd be a good time to try them out.

Zoe No, Tab. We're risking enough as it is. If the Chippies see us with phones that work, we'd never see them again.

Tab Whatever.

They continue with their work for a moment. Zoe stops.

Zoe Are you sure we're going to be all right, Tab? If we're caught on Friday, my dad'll send me for deletion.

Tab We'll have to make sure we're not then.

Zoe What do you do there?

Tab Dance. Have a few drinks.

Zoe Alcohol?

Tab Zoe, don't tell me you've never been drunk before?

Zoe I had a carton of cider with my grandma once.

Tab You little raver. (*Pause*) Just think, in a couple of days' time, you could be the proud owner of a new Chippy boyfriend.

Zoe Pack it in!

Tab Strange things happen once you're over the border.

Zoe Sickening things more like.

Tab Chippy lads are great, Zoe, dead rough and ready.

Zoe Pack it in, Tab.

Tab Fancy kissing one, though.

Zoe Gross!

Tab . . . a long, smoochy-feely snogging sesh.

Zoe Can we get on now, please? You'll be giving us both nightmares.

Tab . . . salt and vinegar aftershave.

Zoe I feel sick.

Tab Oh yes, we could take one of these on Friday . . . bang in the City codes, then spend all night chatting to our sexy Chippy boyfriends. Mmm . . .

Zoe Shut up now!

Tab Relax, will you?

Zoe If anything happened we'd fail the assignment . . .

Tab Zoe?

Act One, Scene Six

Zoe What?

Tab It's called a joke?

Zoe Sorry. I'm just a bit nervous, I suppose. Is that a new TV?

Tab Yeah.

Zoe Would your dad mind if we had it on?

Tab No.

Zoe Where's the remote?

Tab Zoe, please. You're not in Chippyville just yet. This *is* the latest model. (*Speaks to the TV*) Operate. Previous Channel.

Blue light flickers across their faces as stage light fades.

Once more, we hear the Youthopia *theme music. Lights fade down slightly on Tab and Zoe. Blue light flickers across their faces as Nigel and Norma appear on the main screen.*

Norma Welcome back. If you were watching this afternoon, you may have seen our 'Community Executioner work experience offer'. Quite a few of you must have done, as our lines have been completely jammed. Sadly, all the places have now gone so please be a responsible citizen and put your receivers down . . .

Nigel (*finger to his ear*) I'm sorry to interrupt you there, Norma. We have an urgent bulletin. There's been a terrible catastrophe at the Border Gate. We're going straight over to Felicity who has more.

Cut to Outside Broadcast. Felicity stands in close up.

Felicity Thanks, Nige. What a hideous spectacle. Once again, mindless violence has erupted on the other side of the border. You may remember meeting Edward and Pippa earlier today? They were planning to spend an evening with an Inner City family? Only moments ago, I'm shocked to announce, they had to be rushed into the Silverdale Medical Facility after suffering a brutal attack. (*Pauses to wipe away a tear*) They had only been in there five minutes before the family turned on them like a pack of savage animals. Lieutenant Pohlman here is one of the brave DS protectors who helped to save their lives. Lieutenant . . .

Camera pulls out to reveal Lieutenant Pohlman.

. . . What exactly happened?

Pohlman The attack was planned, Felicity. The family had obviously been hoping to kill Pippa and Edward. If it hadn't been for my team, they wouldn't have made it.

Felicity And the family?

Pohlman We had no choice, I'm afraid.

Felicity Thanks, lieutenant. We plan to bring you a further report, once our brave victims are out of the operating theatre. This is Felicity McColgan for *Youthopia* news. Back to the studio. . .

Lights fade back up on Tab and Zoe.

Zoe Tab?

Tab Hmm?

Zoe About Friday . . .?

Scene Seven

Evening of Friday the 4th. An Inner City street at approaching 8 p.m. Lawson stands by a flickering street light not far from the entrance to the Blue Moon Club. We hear a thudding beat escaping from the doors and, from time to time, people try to get past a menacing bouncer. Enter Zena. She looks around, then joins Lawson.

Lawson You OK?

Zena (*not looking at him*) Yeah. So where are we?

Lawson On very thin ice. It should have been incognito. Cal's gunning for Sampson.

Zena He didn't take it too well then?

Lawson You could say that.

Zena Does he suspect you?

Lawson Doubt it. There's gonna be trouble over this one, Zena.

Zena It had to be done, Dave. You don't need that kind of firepower to liberate a few prisoners.

Lawson It's more than a few . . .

Zena Nonetheless, if we'd let him get away with it we could have had a civil war on our hands.

Mick appears behind Zena.

Lawson Watch out.

Lawson holds Zena in a sudden embrace. Mick walks on.

Zena What was that for?

Lawson He's one of the DRED men. And I wanted to.

Bright headlamps sweep over the stage as a car horn blasts over loud music.

. . . You should go now. Please, be careful.

Zena squeezes Lawson's hand, kisses him on the cheek then slips into the darkness. We hear car doors slamming. Enter Larry in a snazzy-looking suit. Exit Lawson.

Larry Here's Larry!

Enter Tim, Tab and Zoe followed by Ned, putting the car keys into his pocket.

Tab (*shouting to Larry*) Get here, you pillock.

Zoe Tab, you've gone all common?

Tab 'When in Chippyville . . .' Let them think you're a nice girl, Zoe, and you've had it.

Ned (*to Larry*) What do you think you're playing at?

Larry Letting them know their peanuts have arrived.

Tim He's drunk already.

Zoe What have peanuts got to do with anything?

Tab It's their word for money.

Larry We've got it, they want it.

Zoe So what stops them from just taking it?

Larry Luck.

Tab Not all Chippies are thieves, Zoe.

Larry Just most of them.

They've reached the entrance. The Bouncer allows a group of Chippy kids through, then stands in the way of Tab's gang.

Bouncer (*to Larry*) Going somewhere, miss?

Ned (*stepping in front with a wad of notes*) Five of us and we expect to leave this dump with smiles on our faces (*holds out another note*) . . . got it?

Bouncer (*takes the note. Looks at Zoe*) So who's the Princess?

Zoe Zoe . . .

Tab (*digging Zoe in the ribs*) None of your soddin' business.

Tim Yeah, eyes off, she wouldn't touch you with a transmitter mast.

Act One, Scene Eight

Ned You gonna let us in or do we take this to some other place?

The Bouncer steps aside and they go in. Zoe is the last. He gives Zoe the eye as she slips past him, trying to look hard. The bouncer grunts at her, Zoe darts into place.

Scene Eight

Continues from the previous scene. Inside the Blue Moon. It's packed. There's a make-shift bar, a dance area and a shabby table with chairs around it. The clientele sway about to hypnotic music. Daz and Mick are at the bar.

Mick Not much talent in here tonight.

Daz Nor any other night either. Want owt?

Mick Keeping a clear head, mate. I'll get *you* one. (*Shouts*) Shaker!

The barman leaves the people he's serving and goes straight over to Mick.

. . . glass of water and a Brain-Drain for young Daz here.

Daz I shouldn't be drinking, Mick.

Mick Make it a large one, Shaker . . . Put a cherry in it an' all. I think he's going soft on us.

Shaker prepares the drinks.

Daz Thanks for sorting this, mate.

Mick He took a bit of persuading. Not nervous, are you?

Daz	Nah, I'm fine.
Mick	Your ex is in tonight, yer know?
Daz	Roz?
Mick	Yeah. I seen her by the bogs.
Daz	That's all I need.

Enter Tab, Ned, Tim, Larry and Zoe. They huddle together in another part of the club.

Mick	Aye, aye. Royalty's in. What's that prat wearing?
Daz	My fist if he tries anything, right in the kisser, eh Mick?

Daz spots Zoe, he follows her with his eyes.

Shaker	Brain-Drain and glass of the old blue stuff. Got company, have we?
Mick	(*pointing to Daz*) Interview.
Shaker	On the house, Mick. (*Winks*)
Mick	(*handing Daz the drink*) There you go, mate. (*Shouts*) Daz!
Daz	(*takes the drink, still looking over at Zoe*) Oh, thanks.
Mick	Yeah.

Our attention is taken to the other side of the room.

Tim	(*to Zoe*) Great, isn't it?
Zoe	It's horrible, Tim. I can't believe you risk your necks to come in here.
Tim	Everyone says that the first time.
Zoe	You've been before as well?
Tim	Yeah, loads.
Tab	(*pushing in*) You're not impressed then?
Zoe	On the contrary, it's simply charming, Tabitha. I particularly love the 'sticky carpet' effect. No wonder none of them can dance.

Act One, Scene Eight

Tab   Yes, they put glue on the floors to stop all the Subby girls from escaping.

Larry   (*to Tab, pointing at Zoe*) She getting the drinks in then?

Zoe   (*to Larry*) It looks like you've had enough.

Tab   Right, it's initiation time, Askew. Virgins get the first round in.

Larry   Not many of them in here.

Tab   Looks like it's you then.

Zoe   Hilarious, Tab. I'm not going over there.

Tab   Yes you are. You'll be fine, just get it over with.

Zoe   What do you all want?

Tab   Ask for Lobotomisers.

Zoe   What are they?

Ned   You don't want to know.

Zoe makes her way to the bar. The music lowers slightly and the lights cross-fade from the bar to two men standing with their backs to the audience. We are in the club toilet (which has a large window). The men are using the urinals. One of them finishes then heads for the door, bumping into Mick as he enters with a glass of water. The accident causes Mick to spill some of it.

Mick   Watch it, idiot?

The first man leaves. Second man turns around. It's Cal.

Cal   Is he here yet?

Mick   He is, Cal, yeah. (*Looks apprehensive*)

Cal   So what's the face for?

Mick   I don't know if I trust him, Cal.

Cal   Del was the best we ever had. If this lad's half the man his brother was, I want him in.

Mick I know all that . . .

Cal Then get over it.

Music fades up and the lights switch back to reveal the bar. Tab's lot have found a table across the room. Zoe is being served. Daz is at the bar also, occasionally turning to look at her.

Zoe (*handing cash over*) Keep the change, thanks.

Roz Get a load of her! Flash little Subby cow. (*To Zoe*) You think you're something, don't yer?

Zoe Sorry.

Roz (*ridiculing*) 'Sorry'.

Zoe I expected them to cost a lot more, I wasn't trying to show off . . .

Roz We know all about being generous, don't we, girls?

Her mates chip in.

. . . give our last drop o' blue stuff away we would.

Roz takes one of Zoe's drinks from the bar and spits into it.

. . . There you go.

She passes it to a friend who does the same. This friend inadvertently hands the glass to Daz.

. . . Look who it isn't. Hiya, Daz babe.

Daz Roz.

Roz We're collecting for the Subby. Wanna make a donation?

Daz No thanks.

Daz deliberately spills some of the drink over Roz.

Roz Watch it, you idiot.

Daz Soz, Roz. Maybe you can get yer Subby boyfriend to lick it off for yer. (*Puts his drink on* *the tray with those Zoe has just bought*) Have mine, love.

Zoe (*surprised but going along with it*) Thanks.

Daz (*whispers to Zoe*) My name's Darren.

Roz Don't tell me you fancy that thing?

Daz (*handing the 'spit drink' to Roz*). You might as well take this. (*To Zoe*) Shall we join the others?

Daz picks up the tray from the bar.

Zoe Why not. (*Looks from Roz to Daz*) Darren.

Zoe leads the way, thrilled with herself. Daz follows with her tray of drinks. Tim is talking to Ned over at their table.

Tim Are you seeing anyone, Ned?

Ned I can't. My dad's promised me to his boss's daughter.

Tim Do you know her?

Ned We've met a couple of times.

Tim Do you like her, though?

Ned I prefer her to the thought of living here full-time.

Tim They wouldn't.

Ned She's a powerful woman.

Tim Who?

Ned His boss, the Super. (*Pause*) So how about you?

Tim There's someone I like. She doesn't know I exist though.

Ned You should tell her then.

Tim She's a friend. At least now I get to talk to her. If I asked her to go out with me I'd probably never see her again.

Ned You shouldn't put yourself down.

Tim Hardly one of the 'in' crowd, though, am I?

Ned You're a lot better than you think you are. Ask her, mate. You might be surprised.

Tab approaches them.

Tab (*to Tim*) Gonna have a dance with me later, Tim?

Larry He can't dance to save his life. I will if you're desperate.

Tab Suicidal more like!

Zoe arrives.

Larry (*reacting to her not carrying the drinks*) I don't believe this. We've been waiting hours. Did you let some Chippy nick them or something?

Zoe No . . .

Tab Come on, I'll go with you this time.

Zoe There's no need, Tab.

Daz appears with the tray of drinks.

. . . This is Darren.

Daz smiles uncomfortably. Zoe puts the drinks on the table. The gang can't believe it.

. . . He offered to carry them over for me.

Larry That's not all he offered, I bet.

Zoe (*to Daz, holding one of the drinks*). Wasn't this one yours?

Daz Keep it.

Mick appears and whispers to Daz. Daz leaves. Zoe's disappointed.

Mick (*to Zoe*) It's all right, love, you can have me if you want.

Mick leaves. They laugh.

Tab So much for giving yourself nightmares. (*Raising her glass*) Shall we?

All except Zoe drink.

Come on, Zoe.

Act One, Scene Eight

Zoe It was that Darren lad's, I don't even know what it is.

Tab Get it down yer. It might be a love potion.

Zoe sniffs at her drink, looks at the others then takes a tentative sip. After a little shudder she decides she likes it and takes a big gulp of the stuff. The others cheer. Larry spots a beautiful girl (Mel).

Larry Not bad. Not bad at all!

Tim Stronger than normal, aren't they?

Larry I'm talking about that. (*Points to Mel*) She's smiling at me, look!

Tab (*to Zoe*) She's probably got wind.

Larry (*gesturing to the girl*) Come on, sit here . . .!

Mel laughs.

Larry Gagging for it.

Zoe She's being friendly, that's all.

Ned Leave it out, Larry.

Larry You're jealous, mate, that's your trouble.

The action reverts back to the men's toilet. Cal is drinking his glass of water. Daz looks around nervously, he doesn't recognise Cal.

Cal Your brother meant a lot to me.

Daz Are you Cal?

Cal How old are you?

Daz Fifteen. I've been waiting years for this, Cal.

Cal Why?

Daz It's what our Del wanted.

Cal What about you? What do you want?

Daz I wanna fight.

Cal You could end up the same way as your brother. Doesn't that bother you?

Daz No. Del died for the best reason there is. When it's my turn, I wannit to be worth somethin'.

Cal This isn't about dying, Barraclough. (*Finishes his glass of water*)

Back to the club. The gang's Lobotomisers are starting to take effect. Zoe and Tab are dancing on a table, Larry is making a spectacle of himself on the dance floor. Ned arrives with another round of drinks.

Zoe Thanks, Ned. (*Gets stuck into her drink*) They're like little lifts.

Tab What are?

Zoe These. Every mouthful. Like a hot little lift. Going up! (*Takes a gulp*) Going down! (*And another*) You can feel it warming everything. (*Giggles*) All your areas.

Tab How many have you had?

Zoe (*takes another swig*) We'll have to be careful though, Tab. I think there might be drugs in these.

Tab So where's your lover boy, I thought it was his job to warm you up tonight?

Zoe Don't be so disgusting, Tab. He was just being kind. They are people, you know.

Tab Sorry. Forgot you were a Chippy lover all of a sudden.

Tab goes to join Larry on the dance floor. Zoe performs free-style on the table. Larry performs dubious dance moves that force Tab away from him. The girl he spotted earlier is dancing with her boyfriend, Jim. Larry's moves become ridiculously suggestive.

Larry (*to Mel*) Fancy a bit of passion, love?

Mel laughs.

Act One, Scene Eight

. . . How about a drink then? Drink! You! Drink?

Mel No thanks.

Larry It's free! Your gorilla can have one an' all if he wants.

Jim What did he say?

Larry Chill out, Chippy.

Jim I wanna know what yer said.

Larry Hard to explain, mate. I was talking in English.

Jim looks angry. Larry attempts even fancier dance moves. People in the club are gathering around to watch.

The action moves back to the toilet.

Cal Ever shot anyone?

Daz Not yet. But there's a first time for everything, I suppose.

Cal takes a gun out.

Cal Kill the girl.

Daz Which one?

Cal The Subby tart. The one you've been drooling over through there.

Daz What has she done?

Cal She's got to you, by the look of things.

Daz The only good Subby is a dead Subby.

Cal I'm glad we agree.

Cal hands his gun over.

. . . No time like the present.

Daz Right.

There's a loud crash and then a scream. Cal jumps out of the window. The music in the club has stopped. Daz tucks the gun into his jeans.

Back in the club, Jim has Larry pinned to the floor.

Larry I'm sorry. I was only having a laugh.

Jim Have this one on me.

Jim hits Larry in the face. Zoe runs over and tries to pull Jim away. Larry breaks free and runs out of the club. Ned and Tim step in to help Zoe, who is now in Larry's place.

Jim Enjoying yourself, are yer . . . having a good time? (*Shouts*) I said, are yer having a good t . . .?

Zoe (*crying*) Yes!

Jim Must like it rough then.

Mel Don't, Jim.

Jim Stay out of it.

Drags Zoe up from the floor.

. . . Thought you'd come laugh at the Chippy blokes, did yer?

Zoe No . . .

Jim You and yer Subby mates. Should give you something to remember us by. Sommat to show yer folks, eh?

Takes out a knife and holds it to Zoe's face. Ned steps forward, he's holding a wad of cash.

Ned Please. I'm sure we can sort this without the need for violence.

Jim Nah, we like a bit of violence, don't we?

Zoe screams as he threatens her again. Tim and Tab get their money out.

Ned Take it.

Tim Just let her go, she hasn't done anything.

Jim Get the peanuts, Macka.

Macka advances towards Ned. He's about to take the cash when Daz appears holding Cal's gun.

Daz I don't think so.

Jim Daz?

Daz Let her go, Jim. This one's mine.
Jim Who says?
Daz (*points gun at Jim*) This does.
Zoe Please!
Jim Shut it!
Daz (*to Ned*) You! Hand it over. And theirs. (*Shouts*) Come on, move it!

Ned takes the cash from Tim and Tab, then slowly approaches Daz. Daz snatches the cash. Tension fills the air. Daz holds everyone in their positions with the point of his gun. All we hear is Zoe crying. Macka makes a move towards Daz, but he's thwarted by the gun being pointed at him.

Jim You can't take us all out.

Daz takes a huge breath then throws the cash into the air. In the commotion, he snatches Zoe from Jim.

Daz (*shouting to Tim, Ned and Tab*) This way!

Daz drags Zoe through the crowd, the others follow.

Scene Nine

Continues from previous scene. In the street, at the back of the club. Tab, Ned and Tim appear from a back-alley. Larry is crouched in a corner.

Larry You made it!
Ned Get to the car.
Tab What about Zoe?

Ned Get to the car, damn it!

Ned, Tim, Tab and Larry exit. Zoe and Daz enter.

Daz Are you OK?

Zoe I thought I was gonna die.

Daz You nearly did. Best get after yer mates.

Zoe Why did you help us?

Daz Dunno.

Zoe Thanks, Darren.

Daz Yeah.

They stare at each other for a moment. Zoe turns to go, Daz grabs her hand and pulls her back.

. . . Call me Daz!

Daz leans in slightly as though to kiss her. Zoe lingers for a second then pulls away. She looks around for the others then turns back to face Daz. After taking a deep breath, she kisses him.

Zoe Thanks, Daz.

Zoe runs away. Daz watches her as the lights go down.

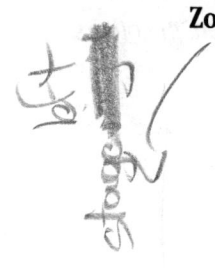

ACT TWO

Scene One

It's Friday the 11th. With another 'clunk', Gran appears in a sterile tube of light. She is stretching.

Gran Those who have courage to love . . . (*stretch*) should also have courage to suffer. (*Stretch*) My mother used to say that. I didn't have a clue what she meant of course. (*Stretch*) You can't choose who, you can't choose when and the worst part is, we're expected to fool ourselves into thinking differently. (*Sits down*) These days you're lucky if you get to do any choosing at all. It's all about money now. Families doing favours for each other. (*Pause*) I didn't marry. My son was born out of wedlock. It was still legal back then, but plenty of people pretended to be outraged. Mostly the ones with skeletons of their own, as usual. I've never been much bothered with what people thought. It's not so easy when you're young, though.

Lights down.

Scene Two

Monday the 7th. Morning. At Zoe's school. Mrs Moncrieff is rehearsing a short play that she's written for assembly. The cast are wearing homemade costumes and are a little unsure of their performances.

Mrs Moncrieff   Get it right this time, there's no excuse. You've had weeks to learn the script. Tabitha . . .?

Tab   Yes, Miss Moncrieff?

Mrs Moncrieff   You are supposed to be playing a savage . . .

Tab   Yes, Miss.

Mrs Moncrieff   Make it look like one.

Tab   But I don't know what they do.

Mrs Moncrieff   Grunt or something. Beginners please.

Tim plays a keyboard as their Narrator takes his place.

Narrator   Once long ago, our beautiful community was threatened by a menacing addiction. For many years, our townspeople had taken care of the sick, they had been provided for, their every need met. This was our first mistake. We gave without expectation, they took and expected more.

Mrs Moncrieff   Very good, Justin.

A group of 'Savages' enter the space. Tab plays Savage One and gently pushes one of the others as she enters.

Savage One   Get owt me road, yer mucky article, I wanna get me hands on some free grub!

Savage Two   Yeah, me an' all. Why should all the posh types have everything?

Savage Three   Just cos they've got jobs and pay taxes.

The Savages mime eating crops from a field. Enter a wealthy landowner.

Landowner   Hey, you despicable gang of heathens, stop stealing my crops and destroying our society.

Act Two, Scene Two

Savage One Get knotted, yer snob. We want what's ours and we's gonna take it.

Savage Two Maybe he'd like to try stoppin' us.

Landowner Violence never solved anything. If you were intelligent and knew a good thing when you had it, you'd stop right at this instant.

Enter two further characters: one is the Leader, in a balaclava and swishing cape; the other is Sampson, played by Zoe, stooped and grotesque.

Leader I am the leader of these poor hungry people. I'm here to see they get everything they want.

Landowner You are nothing but a callous fearmonger. Who is this creature?

Leader My trusty accomplice, Sampson. Let them fill their empty bellies, they need your potatoes to make their chips.

The Savages bow down to the leader, Sampson kicks a couple of them. We hear a couple of 'ooches' and 'ouches'.

Landowner These people can't be hungry, I gave them a whole lot of food only yesterday.

Sampson I say we murder him.

Savage Two But if we kill him, we'd have to grow the potatoes ourselves.

Leader I have the answer. We enslave the selfish landowner and make him work for us!

Savages cheer.

. . . That way, we get to keep everything without having to earn it. Take him away, Sampson.

Sampson Can I torture him, Master?

Leader Yes, don't kill him though, he has much to do for us.

Savages laugh heartily. Sampson drags Landowner away.

... Come, faithful subjects, there are many others for us to kill.

Sampson stops in his tracks.

Sampson Wait, I've got a better idea. Why don't we just kill ourselves?

Mrs Moncrieff Zoe, if we can't remember our lines we ask for a prompt.

Sampson (*taking her costume off*) Or failing that, we could build a wall round all the poor areas, tell lies about the people living there to make everyone afraid of them, then live happily ever after!

The rest of the class are in shock, they can't believe Zoe's doing this.

Mrs Moncrieff Zoe Askew, what on earth do you think you are doing?

Zoe This is horrible, Miss . . .

Mrs Moncrieff What do you expect, it's about the terrorist movement.

Zoe Your twisted version of it.

Mrs Moncrieff I think you owe everyone an apology.

Zoe I think *you* do. This is pure propaganda. It's nothing short of brainwashing.

Mrs Moncrieff How dare you! Tabitha?

Tab Yes, Miss.

Mrs Moncrieff Learn the part of Sampson. Zoe doesn't deserve a leading role.

Zoe I didn't want it in the first place, neither does Tab.

Tab Zoe?

Zoe . . . It wasn't anything like this. Poor people

	were denied their rights so that the rich people could get even richer. That's what we should be saying.
Mrs Moncrieff	Don't be so preposterous!
Zoe	Stop trying to brainwash us then!
Mrs Moncrieff	They denied themselves through a regime of fear and violence. They are terrorists, Zoe Askew, they murder people . . .
Zoe	And we don't? Call them what you want, Chippies, Terrorists, Savages even, they're still people. Just like you or me and anyone that says different is either a liar, a coward or both.

The rest of the class look at Zoe as though she has just murdered someone.

Mrs Moncrieff Follow me. We'll see what the Principal has to say about this. This new-found affection of yours may be better placed in an Inner City school.

Zoe is marched out. All except Tim and Tab laugh at her. Members of the class shout 'Chippy lover' and 'Kick-out'.

Scene Three

Same day. Daz is at his school. The room is dark and miserable-looking.

Mr James It doesn't take a genius to know that the Fiftieth Anniversary of the Income Qualification Bill is almost upon us. Taylor?

Taylor What?

Mr James I'd like your opinion.

Taylor It's crap.

Mr James Would this be the Bill or your opinion of it?

Dawn I don't know why we've gotta learn this stuff.

The Bill is what put us all here in the first place. It's like rubbing our noses in it.

Mr James Why do you say that?

Dawn Subbies had all the peanuts in the first place. They was scared in case the likes of us took it from 'em, so they shut us in here.

Mr James According to the Bill, everyone has a right to citizenship so long as they make a contribution, pay taxes in other words . . .

Alex Only Subbies can afford to, though.

Mr James So, what can we do about it?

Daz (*under his breath*) Kill the Subbies.

Mr James Something to say, Barraclough?

Daz No, sir.

A bell sounds. Everyone jumps up.

Mr James . . . The Income Qualification Bill is not the only example of one human society trying to oppress another. Prepare a discussion for tomorrow morning please.

The class leaves. Mr James stops Daz and takes an exercise book from him.

. . . You haven't been yourself lately, Barraclough. Is something bothering you?

Daz No, sir.

Mr James (*reading from the cover of the book*). 'DRED good, Subbies bad. Kill the Subby scum'. This is how people get themselves deleted.

Daz looks away.

. . . It's ignorance, Barraclough.

Daz Chippy, ain't I?

Mr James You join that organisation and, before too long, you're going to have blood on your hands. You may fool yourself into justifying some of it but

Act Two, Scene Three

	somewhere along the line you'll murder someone who's fighting the same battle as you. Are you in the habit of killing friends, Barraclough?
Daz	Subbies and Chippies don't make friends.
Mr James	Have you heard of an organisation called FAIR?
Daz	Yeah. Subby snobs thinking they're great cos they help a couple of poor kids now and then.
Mr James	There's more to it than that.
Daz	Not much. It's a nice bit of charity to make themselves feel better. The best kind of Subby is a dead Subby, FAIR or not.
Mr James	So, what are you going to do, Barraclough? Maybe you should shoot *me*?
Daz	You're OK, sir.
Mr James	You're one of the brightest kids in this place. You've got what it takes to make a difference. Don't waste yourself on this.
Daz	They killed our Del.
Mr James	That's an excuse to go and kill someone else's brother, is it?
	Pause. Mr James looks at the book again.
	. . . Who's this drawing of?
Daz	Dunno, sir.
Mr James	(*reading*) 'Daz 4 *Question mark*'. For someone you don't know, you've certainly paid a lot of attention to detail.
Daz	Can I go please?
Mr James	Yes, you can go. If you have any sense, it'll be straight to this girl of yours. She might help to knock some sense into you. You could even try asking her name, Barraclough?
Daz	(*taking the book back*) Wouldn't have me, sir. (*To himself*) Neither of 'em.

Scene Four

It's Saturday the 12th. Gran appears in the usual fashion.

Gran Imagine you were going to be put on your own, maybe for the rest of your life. What would be the one thing you'd take with you? Difficult, isn't it? People disappear all the time around here. They're lucky if they get to keep the clothes they stand in never mind anything else. But no matter how hard things get for someone, they'll always have what they carry in here (*points to her heart*) and here (*points to her head*). Boundaries don't exist in these places.

Lights come up on Zoe. She's on another part of the stage, and kneeling beside a rocking chair. The chair rocks even though no one is sitting in it. Beside it is a small table on which stands a vase of yellow roses.

Gran stands up.

. . . I don't have a lot of time left. I have to face that. There are things I can't do any more. There are places I'll never see again. If I want to be elsewhere, I have to go there in here (*points to her heart*). Visit a memory. Everyone can do it. Even children have yesterdays.

Gran has made her way over to Zoe and sits in the rocking chair. We are visiting a memory from the evening of Monday the 7th. The sterile light fades away.

Gran . . . You could've been expelled, Zoe.

Zoe It'd have been better if I had. No one's talking to me. Those that are don't want anyone to see them.

Act Two, Scene Four   45

Gran So. What's it all about?

Zoe I didn't like telling lies.

Gran There's more to it than that. I know you, Zoe Askew. Tell me.

Zoe I can't, Grandma.

Gran Can't? What's *so* terrible, you can't tell *me* about?

Zoe I met someone.

Gran You did what? Call the police! It's the end of the world as we know it . . .

Zoe Don't, Grandma.

Gran What's the big problem?

Zoe is reluctant, Gran leans towards her.

. . . Hello?

Zoe It's not a Subby boy.

Gran That's narrowed it down a bit. So, if it's not a Subby boy, that means it's a Chippy boy . . . unless it's a girl of course?

Zoe Grandma!

Gran It happens. So that's it, hmm? A Chippy boy has taken your fancy?

Zoe You don't mind?

Pause. Gran takes a sip from her mug.

Gran When I was sixteen, I worked in a record shop in town. One day a young man came in. Not much older than me. The instant I saw him, my heart kicked so hard I thought I was going to die. I was on cassettes, he wanted a CD. I stood and stared all the time he was in there, taking in every detail. I felt such a floozy.

Zoe You were only looking?

Gran It's more what I was thinking, love. So, the thing he wanted was only on import. We had to order

	it, which meant he had to come back and even better, leave his name and phone number. Gordon Payne. Gorgeous Gordon Payne.
Zoe	(*astonished*) Grandma?
Gran	He was gorgeous. I watched him leave then, taking in every little movement. He reached to grab the door, I tell you, Zoe, I'd have given anything to be that door handle. (*Zoe squirms*) Tuesday. He was coming back on the Tuesday. By this time, I'd convinced myself he was going to sweep in and just want me, wishing he'd asked me those few days before. I was obsessed. I spent the whole week writing his name on pieces of paper. I even devised an equation to prove that he loved me.
Zoe	Is that possible?
Gran	Probably not. It didn't stop me from trying though.
Zoe	Did he come back?
Gran	Oh yes. He came back all right. This was 'it' as far as I was concerned. He'd been pining for me the same as I had for him. He was going to storm into that record shop, declare his undying love and we'd live happily ever after.
Zoe	Had he noticed you, Grandma?
Gran	Had he billyo. He picked his CD up, then walked straight out again, not so much as a glance.
Zoe	You're warning me, right?
Gran	All you can do is wait. If this boy cares for you, he'll find a way of letting you know.
Zoe	Maybe I should find a way of letting him know. I could try and find him?
Gran	Not if it means breaking into the City you couldn't. If something is meant for you, it won't pass by. Leave this one to fate, love.

Act Two, Scene Five   4.

Zoe Forget about it, you mean?

Gran I mean, leave it to fate. You can't make somebody love you, Zoe. (*To herself*) You can't stop them either.

Zoe You always know what to say.

Gran Do you feel a bit better now?

Zoe Yes, thanks.

Gran Me too. (*Beat*) I must be getting over him.

Zoe Gordon?

Gran nods.

. . . After all these years?

Gran I don't give up without a fight, Zoe Askew.

Slowly, the sterile column of light reappears. Gran is there also, she sits with her head in her hands. Lights go down on the scene from her memory, then, with the familiar 'clunk', her small room snaps into darkness.

Scene Five

Tuesday the 8th. Late afternoon. Border gate. Chippy workers are leaving the suburbs for the night. People are queuing to get past two DS officers on the gate. Martha and Connie are getting frisked by DS officers.

Martha Mean and moody this one, eh Connie? (*To Officer Adams*) You've missed a bit.

Officer Adams You wanna be here all night?

Martha Now there's an offer.

Connie	Have you still got that gun in yer britches, Martha?
Martha	Oh yes, a girl's not safe these days. Got one in yours?
Connie	'Fraid not. I think he has though . . .
Officer Mian	That'll do. Go on. Next in line.

Connie and Martha go through. The DS officers continue to search people. Zena and Lawson are further back in the queue. There's a character standing behind them wearing a long, hooded coat.

Lawson	Hard day at the office, dear?
Zena	Not so good for the Wentworths. Do you know Zoe Askew?
Lawson	Yeah, nice kid. She got herself into trouble yesterday.
Zena	You were there, then?
Lawson	No, the word was going round. School caretakers don't miss out on much.
Zena	The Wentworths are getting nervous. They can't risk their Tabitha mixing with a Sympathiser, can they?
Lawson	Might give the game away. Poor kid'll have no one soon, Tab and the Bixby lad are about the only kids that'll talk to her.
Zena	So how's the Sampson hunt?
Lawson	Cal's got everyone mobilised. No leads as yet though. What happened to the guns, Zena?
Zena	We had them destroyed.
Lawson	Cal thinks FAIR might have used them against him.
Zena	Sampson'll have a good laugh at that one.

Lawson and Zena reach the gate. As they walk away, the character in the coat takes his hood down. It's Mick.

Scene Six

Tuesday the 8th. Late afternoon. Zoe, carrying a school bag, approaches the Wentworths' front door. She's a little out of breath and keeps looking behind her. She knocks until Mr Wentworth opens the door.

Zoe Hello, Mr Wentworth. Is Tab around? I've come to work on the phones.

Mr Wentworth I'm sorry, Zoe. She can't see you.

Zoe Is she ill or something?

Mr Wentworth Not exactly.

Zoe It's about what happened in school yesterday, isn't it? I was in a bad mood, that's all. I didn't mean any of what I said. Please, can I come in, Mr Wentworth?

Mr Wentworth Maybe you should go home, Zoe.

Zoe I can't. There's a gang waiting for me. They're at the end of your drive. If I go back, they'll have me.

Mr Wentworth (*takes a card from his wallet*) This opens the gate at the far side of the grounds. Follow the path there. It leads onto the waste ground. It's a longer route, but you can get home without them seeing you. Quickly now.

Zoe What's going o . . .?

Mr Wentworth Just get yourself home, Zoe.

Scene Seven

Tuesday the 8th. Late afternoon. Daz is in a tunnel.

Daz This has to be the stupidest thing I've ever done. Seems like miles and still no sign you're going the right way. You're an idiot, Daz. Good job Del's not here . . .

There's a shrill squeak as Daz steps on something.

. . . If I don't get through, at least there's sommat to eat down here.

The lights cross-fade from the tunnel to the waste ground. Zoe is angry and confused.

Zoe What have I done? It's not as if they know about the Blue Moon. Unless Tabby's told them? She wouldn't do that, it's more than her life's worth. All this for giving Moncrieff a few home truths. I can't believe it. (*Looking around her*) I thought Chippies were the ones with lynch mobs, not Subby kids. (*Pause*) The things they were shouting! If they used that sort of language in school, they'd be deleted. It's all right to say it to a 'Chippy lover'. (*Pause for thought*) Dad was right. I'm a Chippy lover! I'm a Sympathiser and an outcast like he said.

Lights cross-fade, back to Daz in the tunnel. Daz is talking to his dead brother.

Daz You told me 'bout this place, eh Del? Wonder if it stank as much in the days you used it? Wonder how many times you was here? Maybe on this spot. Dragging Subby prisoners back for Cal. I bet you were never as scared as I am now. I'd never have told you that when you was

alive. Stupid i'n't it? I wish you was still here
Del, you know that, don't yer? I bet you'd tell
me I was stupid and make me turn back, eh? I
reckon you'd be right an' all.

Lights cross-fade back to the waste ground. Zoe is sitting on a rock.

Zoe What if Grandma was right? She usually is. All of this for nothing. All of this because I got it into my stupid head that some lad who couldn't care less fancies me. How stupid can you get? (*Pause*) He did say to call him Daz. He did say that. I bet he's said that to hundreds of us. All waiting in line for scraps of his attention. (*Pause*) Could be worse, I suppose. At least he didn't throw up when I kissed him.

Back to Daz.

Daz This is it. Light at the end of the tunnel. How corny can you get? It'll be sealed off knowing my luck. Either that or I'll have taken the wrong turn. I could be back in the City for all I know.

The attention goes back to Zoe, she's now worked herself into a frenzy.

Zoe There was one at the bar even! Roz '. . . think you're it, don't yer'. If that's what he likes in a girlfriend I've got no chance. I can't even spit straight. (*Mimicking Roz*) 'We're right generous, us Chippies, aren't we, girls?'

Not too far away, a manhole cover opens. As Zoe proceeds, Daz's arms appear.

'. . . you don't fancy her, do yer?' (*Hacks and spits*)

Daz lifts himself out of the ground, blinking in the daylight. He looks to see where the voice is coming from.

'. . . doing a collection'. (*Hack, spit*) 'Want to

make a donation, Daz babe!' (*Hacks and spits again*)

Daz sees Zoe. He can hardly believe his eyes.

. . . I'll give her a donation!

Daz Is that really you?

Zoe Ahhh! . . . (*Stops in her tracks*) Darren?

Daz Daz.

Zoe What are you doing here? (*To herself*) . . . I'm dreaming. I must be. This is too weird. They must have caught me, that's it. I'm really in a gutter somewhere with my teeth missing.

Daz You look fine to me.

Zoe This is real?

Daz I am.

They look at each other.

. . . Do you want me to go?

Zoe (*shouts*) No! (*Trying to be cool*) Stay, if you like. What *are* you doing here?

Daz Looking for a Subby.

Zoe Looks like you've found one.

Daz I'm not going to hurt you.

Zoe I know. You saved my life, remember.

Daz I can't believe you're here. I never thought I'd find you this easy.

Zoe (*amazed*) You were *looking* for me?

Daz Yeah. Weird, i'n't it? What you called?

Zoe Chippy lover mostly . . . My name's Zoe.

Daz Sounds like a little animal.

Zoe Better than a washing powder.

Daz What?

Zoe It doesn't matter.

Daz You spit good for a Subby lass.

Scene Eight

Still early evening of Tuesday the 8th. Domestic Services HQ. Lieutenant Pohlman and Sergeant Dawes have just finished an interrogation. Abbo's body lies slumped in a chair. Pohlman drinks from a hip flask.

Pohlman Faithful to the last.

Offers a drink to Dawes, who refuses.

Dawes Are you sure he was DRED, sir? He looks a bit young to me.

Pohlman (*speaks into a recording device*) Interview terminated at fourteen hundred hours. Suspect withheld information. (*To Dawes*) If I didn't know better, Dawes, I'd say you were sympathising. (*Shouts*) Get in here.

Enter two DS officers.

. . . Remove it.

The officers remove Abbo's body.

. . . He's DRED all right. Takes an idiot of conviction to take that kind of punishment.

A third DS officer enters.

Officer Blake Lieutenant?

Pohlman What?

Officer Blake We've had a tip-off, sir. The identity of a FAIR activist.

Pohlman You have my attention, officer.

Officer Blake It's a ringleader by all accounts.

Pohlman This is proving to be a busy day. Get a team together, Dawes. It's time to collect ourselves a Sympathiser. Who gave us the lead?

Officer Blake	He claimed to be from DRED, lieutenant. We couldn't get a trace.
Pohlman	Anything else?
Officer Blake	No, sir, just that . . . He did say we'd be doing them a favour.

Scene Nine

Back to the waste ground. Daz and Zoe are both sitting on the rock.

Daz	Was she there that night?
Zoe	Yeah. We're best mates. If it wasn't for Tab I wouldn't have been there.
Daz	Proper Subby name – Wentworth. Same as the builder guy.
Zoe	That's her dad.
Daz	He built half of Silverdale.
Zoe	Yeah, they're loaded.
Daz	Glad to hear it.
Zoe	You must think I'm a right snob.
Daz	If any of my mates' dads was a millionaire, I'd be at their place all the time.
Zoe	Billion.
Daz	What?
Zoe	Billionaire. Sick, isn't it? Money can't buy everything though. Tab still goes to school like the rest of us. She'll never have to work, unless she wants to, mind you. We were supposed to be testing these out this afternoon. (*Takes the phones from her bag*)

Act Two, Scene Nine

Daz They're getting on a bit.

Zoe That's the point, we've upgraded them. We've had to swap a lot of the circuitry, they needed new ports too, well obviously. Sorry. You didn't come here to talk about school, right?

Daz I still can't believe you're here. It must be our Del.

Zoe Del?

Daz My brother. It's like I can feel him around me sometimes. He died. He was in DRED, one of the best they had. Best brother you could have an' all. He used to tell me stuff, secret stuff sometimes, getting me ready.

Zoe You're one of the terrorists?

Daz No.

Zoe Why would you want to join an organisation that goes around killing people?

Daz I never joined. I wanted to, yeah. So would you if you'd grown up on our side . . .

Zoe I wouldn't.

Daz You would, that's all anyone ever talks about. It's a way of making yoursen count for something. I'm telling you, Zoe, you would.

Zoe I've got a mind of my own.

Daz So have I. There's reasons, you know.

Zoe Like what?

Daz I want to get the DS back for what they did to our Del. If you'd ever lost anyone, you'd understand.

Zoe Was he deleted?

Daz In the end. If they're gonna delete a DRED man, you can bet it won't be as soon as they catch him. They took our Del two years ago. He was sixteen. A year older than me now. Some reckon he could still be alive in there.

Zoe That's horrible.

Daz I hope he isn't. I never joined, Zoe.

Zoe Do we have to talk about this?

Daz Maybe we should talk about us.

Zoe There's an us?

Daz Feels like it to me.

Zoe We're so different. We couldn't be more . . .

Daz Opposites attract . . . physics.

Zoe tries to hide her surprise.

. . . Not just Subbies go to school, you know. If you don't want this, I'll go, you'll never see me again.

Zoe No.

Daz You don't mind then?

Zoe I was going to try and find you.

Daz Really?

Zoe My gran told me to wait, she said . . .

Daz (*angry*) Your gran? You've told someone? Zoe, if they know I've seen you, I'll be finished. Are you stupid or something?

Zoe There's no danger, you haven't met my gran. (*Pause*) And don't call me stupid, you sound like my dad.

Daz Sorry.

Pause. Daz sniggers.

Zoe What?

Daz We've just had our first row.

Zoe smiles. Daz looks into the distance.

. . . See that tower block?

Zoe Where?

Daz (*points over Zoe's shoulder*) Just there, sticking out above the others, look.

Act Two, Scene Nine

Zoe I see it.
Daz That's where I live.
Zoe How far do you think it is?
Daz Couple of miles, maybe three.

Daz now has his arm round Zoe.

Zoe If you told people all this, they'd never believe it. There are places in the world now where we could be together and no one would bat an eyelid. It's like something out of a book.
Daz Dystopia.

Zoe looks at Daz both confused and amazed. Heavy footsteps are heard.

Officer Adams (*off*) Couple of kids . . .
Officer Mian (*off*) Best check 'em out.
Zoe Daz! They must be on a patrol.
Daz I'll have to get back, Zoe.
Zoe How will I see you?
Daz I'll find a way. Do you drive?
Zoe No, you've got to be seventeen. Ahh!

She remembers the phones and takes one from her bag. It has a box crudely taped to it and looks homemade. She starts to make adjustments.

Daz What are you doing?
Zoe Just a second . . . I want you to take this.
Daz No good to me, is it?
Zoe We got hold of the codes. It should work, even in the City. We didn't get to test them, obviously . . . There.

Hands the phone over.

Daz What's your number?
Zoe I'll call you. Keep it hidden, Daz.

Daz I wanna stay here with you.

Zoe kisses Daz. They hug for a moment. Enter Officer Blake. He's armed.

. . . No!

Zoe What?

Daz He's standing over the tunnel entrance. Scarper, Zoe.

Zoe What about you?

Daz Forget about me. Run for it.

Daz steals a final kiss then runs away. Enter Officer Adams who spots him.

. . . Go!

Daz stands. Officer Adams aims his gun.

Officer Adams Freeze!

Daz runs in the opposite direction to Zoe. Lights fade to the sound of machine-gun fire.

Scene Ten

It's Saturday the 12th. The sterile light comes on with a 'clunk'. Gran is sitting in her chair.

Gran Even the strongest people cry sometimes. There's a lot to cry about. Then again, even the most horrible situation might happen for a reason. People have a wonderful knack for reason. If you can sit there and honestly tell me you've never fallen out with anyone then this won't involve you. For the honest ones among us, just take a minute. There's two sides to every argument and the other side think they're

just as right as you. Where do you start?
Fighting? Killing? A spot of humiliation maybe?
You might even join a group, surround yourself
with people who believe in the same things as
you. We've all done that as well. This comes as
a bit of a shock to people sometimes, but I'll tell
you anyway. You've already joined the biggest
group there is. Like it or not, we are members
of one another.

Scene Eleven

Tuesday the 8th. Evening. Zoe's house. The light from the TV flickers across the faces of Gerald and Amanda as they watch more of the Youthopia *programme. This time we hear the report, rather than watching it on the screen. Felicity is heard over the sound of a helicopter.*

Felicity (*off*) The scene is one of horror. Only moments ago, we set off in this helicopter to see if we could catch a glimpse of the brutal murderer. Apparently he's used an old tunnel leading straight into Silverdale from the border regions.

Norma (*off*) Were there any bodies found, Felicity?

Felicity (*off*) I believe so, Norma. Apparently a group of young girls were playing ball on the area of waste land when the killer attacked. An eyewitness said they saw one of the girls run away, the others were savagely killed by this Chippy maniac. We have the pictures from the chase now.

A door slams. Enter Zoe. She looks at the screen and gasps.

. . . These pictures were taken from a DS camera at the scene of the crime. The attacker, running to the left of your screen there, is approximately five foot ten inches in height with dark brown or black hair and thought to be concealing a number of dangerous weapons . . .

Lights up in the Askew living room.

Zoe What's this? Who's been attacked?

Gerald Decided to join us, have you?

Amanda A Chippy boy was chased from the waste ground. We were worried about you, Zoe. It happened not far from Tabitha's house.

Gerald DS know what they're doing. You worry too much.

Zoe (*covering herself*) Tab and I did hear something. On the waste ground you say?

Amanda Yes, only a few hundreds yards away.

Zoe What did they say? Did they catch him?

Gerald If you both shut your mouths for a minute, we might find out. There he is, look (*pointing at the screen*). Cowards when it comes down to it, hopping away like a scared little rabbit. Ah, missed!

Amanda You would be with all those guns pointing at you. (*Looking at Zoe's shoes*) Zoe, we've just had the carpets done.

Gerald Look at him go!

Amanda We thought one of the bullets must've knocked the phones out or something. We tried to call, you see.

Zoe The Wentworths are having repairs done.

Amanda Shoes?

Zoe (*takes them off*) Sorry. I came across the school field.

Amanda	Your father was going to come and pick you up, we were waiting for the bulletin to finish. Still, you're back now.
Gerald	(*still watching the TV*) He got away? I don't believe it. How can they lose someone in this day and age?
	Zoe starts to cry. Amanda hugs her.
Amanda	They should keep all of this violence off the television, it's not nice.
Gerald	The more we know the better. Keep your friends close and your enemies closer.
Zoe	Can I go to my room please?
Mum	Course you can, love. Give me those.
Zoe	(*handing Amanda her shoes*) Thank you.
	Exit Zoe.
Gerald	Wonders never cease, she's found a few manners at last.

Scene Twelve

Wednesday the 9th. Midday. An interrogation room at DRED HQ. There is a figure tied to a chair with its back to us (it is Zena). Cal and Mick enter. Mick carries a tray with the glass and bottle of water.

Cal	(*to figure in chair*) It's time we had a little chat.
Zena	Murderer.
	Mick goes to slap the prisoner. Cal stops him.
Cal	You must be feeling very proud. Do you have

any idea how much your interfering has cost? Members of FAIR are obviously not interested in freedom . . .

Zena   It had nothing to do with freeing people . . .

Cal puts his hand over her mouth.

Cal   You should do yourself a favour.

Nods to Mick, who pours a glass of water.

. . . You have the chance to save yourself.

Mick hands the water to Cal. Cal spins the chair around to reveal Zena to the audience and holds the glass in front of her.

. . . Tell me what I need to know and I will be tolerant. Do you want to live?

Zena   Not here I don't.

Cal   (*to Mick*) Find Shaker.

Lights cross-fade to a Domestic Services interrogation chamber. It is the same day. Two DS officers drag a hooded man into the room. (It is Lawson.) He struggles free. One of the officers knocks him to the ground. He is then secured to a table. The officers leave the room. A bright light comes on with the familiar-sounding 'clunk', and shines down on Lawson. Enter Sergeant Dawes and Lieutenant Pohlman.

Pohlman   So, we have ourselves a FAIR boy. One of Sampson's little helpers.

Lawson struggles, Pohlman pulls the hood off. The light almost blinds Lawson, he turns his head away from us.

Like that, do you? Aww, doesn't feel much like chatting, Dawes. He'd like to flutter those 'FAIRy' wings and fly away. It's not going to happen though. There's something about wings, I always want to clip them.

Act Two, Scene Twelve

Pohlman and Dawes approach Lawson. The action freezes. Lights cross-fade back to the previous DRED location. Shaker stands over Zena filling a syringe from a small, brown bottle.

Shaker If this won't get her talking, nothing will.

Zena You might as well kill me.

Mick And miss all the fun.

Zena Animal.

Shaker Nice drop of sodium pentathol. Knocks spots off a Lobotomiser. Arm?

Mick holds his arm out.

. . . hers, Mick.

Mick pulls up Zena's sleeve and holds her arm still. Shaker administers the injection.

Shaker Lucky little prisoner. Few peanuts going in there, you know. Couple of minutes we're gonna be all loved up. Giz a kiss.

Zena I'd rather die. You're wasting your time, you do know that?

Cal We'll see.

Cross back to the DS chamber. Lawson's arms hang limp and twisted over the sides of the table.

Pohlman Mind if I call you Dave? (*To Dawes*) What have we got?

Dawes (*reading from a file*) Caretaker at Silverdale High. No previous record. Got a thing going with a Chippy maid. Metcalf they call her. Zena Metcalf. He's kept a low profile, this one.

Pohlman What about the woman?

Dawes Clean. As far as we know. She works for the Wentworths.

Pohlman We should bring her in as well.

Lawson	Leave her alone.
Dawes	We can't find her, sir. She disappeared some time yesterday afternoon.
Pohlman	She's probably dead by now then. Not to worry, eh Dave? She'd be no use to you anyway, not by the time we've finished with you. Unless you want to make it easy for us.
Lawson	Go to hell!
Pohlman	(*to Dawes*) Get the tools.

Scene Thirteen

Wednesday the 9th. Early evening. Zoe's bedroom. Zoe is talking into her mobile phone. Daz's face appears on the screen; from time to time, the image distorts. His face is cut and bruised.

Zoe	. . . I can't believe you got away from them.
Daz	There's two ways into the tunnel. I found the other one just in time.
Zoe	I thought I was never going to see you again, Daz.
Daz	I thought they might have got you an' all. Did you hear the fans?
Zoe	Sorry?
Daz	The 'copters, Zoe.
Zoe	Oh, yeah. It made the headlines this morning. You were on the TV as well. It was on when I got in. They're trying to make out you killed people, Daz.

Act Two, Scene Thirteen

Daz It's what Chippies do, i'n't it? Are they on to you, do you think?

Zoe Doesn't look like it. I want to see you, Daz. I could come to you this time, I saw where the tunnel came out.

Daz You can't, Zoe . . .

Zoe I want to . . .

Daz No. Promise me you won't.

Zoe I thought you'd want to see me . . .

Daz I left a trail so I'd get back, right?

Zoe Yeah?

Daz But cos I used a different way back, I got lost down there, I couldn't find it. I ended up in a DRED house, Zoe, they weren't happy neither.

Zoe But they're on your side?

Daz DRED are on DRED's side. Only them are supposed to know about it.

Zoe How come you knew about it then?

Daz Our Del told me.

Zoe Just tell me which way to go . . .

Daz You don't understand, Zoe. You try and use that tunnel, you're going to end up dead. I thought they were gonna kill me last night. You don't wanna know what they'd do if they found a Subby down there.

Zoe I wish I could be with you.

Daz You're better off where you are.

Zoe Your face looks sore.

Daz I've had worse.

Zoe You should clean that cut, you know.

Daz What with?

Zoe Touch your face, Daz.

Daz What?

Zoe Touch the side of your face.

Clumsily, he puts a hand to his face.

. . . Imagine it's me. This is so wrong. If we'd been born in a different place, just a couple of miles away . . .

Daz is about to take his hand away.

. . . Pretend I'm stroking it better, Daz.

Zoe closes her eyes.

Daz Zoe . . .?

Zoe Don't talk. Just imagine I'm there . . . I'm touching the other side now.

Daz is having difficulty getting into it.

. . . Does that feel nice, Daz?

Pause.

Daz Suppose. I can think of someone better to touch, though.

Scene Fourteen

Back to the DRED interrogation room. Thirty minutes have passed. Zena is now drowsy.

Cal Mick tells me you're friendly with Sampson. Nice bloke, is he?

Zena Not exactly.

Cal I'm glad we agree on something. Where are the weapons, Zena?

Zena Crusher in a scrapyard.

Cal Which scrapyard?

Zena The one with all the flat shooters. (*Laughs*)

Act Two, Scene Fourteen

Mick So how did you get 'em?

Cal Gently does it, Michael, don't want to scare her, do we?

Zena Tried paying for 'em first. FAIR isn't it, got more peanuts than your lot. Dealers wouldn't go for it though. They must be scared of you, Cal. We had to do the swap ourselves.

Cal That can't have been easy, Zena?

Zena Shh. Have to be quiet. Dave helped.

Mick He's taken care of.

Cal gives Mick a dig and mimes 'Shut it!'

Cal And the rest you did on your own, is that right?

Zena I just helped. Mr Wentworth made it all happen.

Cal (*to Shaker*) Are you getting this?

Shaker (*with recording device*) Every word, Cal.

Cross-fade to the DS interrogation chamber. Lawson is hooked up to an electrical device, he's writhing in pain.

Pohlman Nice, isn't it? Like me to up the voltage a little? All you have to do is keep your mouth shut.

Lawson I don't know anything.

Another scream as Pohlman presses the switch.

Pohlman I'd like to believe you, Dave. Hard nut to crack this one. (*Holds his hand out*) Dawes?

Dawes is uncomfortable.

. . . You want me to get it?

Dawes reluctantly hands Pohlman an electric drill. Lights cross back over to DRED.

Zena It's for your own good, Cal. Killing DS isn't going to make anythin' better. Killin' nobody is. They was helping. There's a lot of us, Cal. All you got to do is ask. We'll help you, Cal. FAIR want to stop all this as much as you do.

Cal	I like the sound of that, Zena. Maybe I should talk to Sampson?
Zena	Don't know. Sampson likes to stay secret.
Mick	She's gonna tell us, Cal.
Cal	(*seething whisper*) Shut it! (*To Zena, nice again*) How can I talk to him if I don't know who he is?
Zena	Can't.
Cal	Is it Mr Wentworth, Zena, is Mr Wentworth Sampson?
Zena	(*giggles*) No, silly.
Cal	If I'm going to talk to him, Zena, I have to know his name?
Zena	(*laughs*) I'll whisper.

Cal stoops as Zena whispers in his ear.

Cal	(*to Shaker*) You told me they don't lie with that stuff?
Shaker	It's impossible Cal, 'specially on the dose she's had.
Cal	Unbelievable.
Mick	Has she told you, Cal?
Cal	(*takes a deep, calming breath*) She's told me, yes.
Mick	You want me to finish her off then?
Cal	(*grabs Mick*) She lives.

Cut back to DS. Lawson lies dead on the table. Pohlman is removing blood-stained gloves. He drinks from his hip flask, then offers some to Dawes, who is obviously sickened by what he's just seen. Dawes takes a drink. Pohlman's amused at his reaction.

Scene Fifteen

Thursday the 10th. Late afternoon. Tab and Mr Wentworth are in the garden.

Tab I just want to say goodbye to everyone. It's not such a crime, is it?

Mr Wentworth You can't, Tabitha. I'm sorry.

Tab But this is the first time I've stayed off, they'll want to . . .

Mr Wentworth I said no.

An alarm sounds. They both tense up.

. . . Get inside!

Tab Is it them?

Mr Wentworth Do as you're told.

Exit Mr Wentworth further into the garden. Mrs Wentworth comes from the house.

Mrs Wentworth Someone's opened the back gate. Where's your father?

Tab He went towards the orchard.

Mrs Wentworth You'd better come inside, Tabitha.

Tab I hate this. It's stupid.

Tab and Mrs Wentworth go inside the house.

Mr Wentworth (*off*) You could've got yourself killed, young lady. That gate is protected.

Zoe (*off*) No one would answer the door, Mr Wentworth. I was worried.

Mr Wentworth (*off*) You're not the only one . . .

Enter Mr Wentworth and Zoe.

Zoe Are you going to tell me what's happening?

Mr Wentworth Please, Zoe . . .

Re-enter Tab.

Zoe Not letting me in your house is one thing, but keeping Tab out of school just because of something I said is ridiculous. Everyone's been asking about her. I'm sorry, Mr Wentworth, but I want to see her. Something's going on, I can feel it.

Mr Wentworth It's for your own safety.

Zoe They always say that . . .

Tab He's right, Zoe.

Zoe Tab.

Tab Please, Dad, just for a short while?

Re-enter Mrs Wentworth.

Mrs Wentworth Tabitha, get back inside this instant . . .

Mr Wentworth It's all right, darling. (*To Tab*) Quickly. And Tabitha? . . . Discretion please.

Mr and Mrs Wentworth go inside.

Zoe What was all that about?

Tab We're your friends, Zoe, you have to remember that. I can't say much. Just that there's been some trouble. It's best that we don't see each other.

Zoe This is stupid. I give Moncrieff a couple of home truths and they take it out on you. Listen, I'll tell them tomorrow. I'll tell the Principal it's nothing to do with you.

Tab It isn't to do with you either, Zoe.

Zoe What's going on? Less than a week ago, everything was fine. We take a stupid trip to . . .

Tab Keep your voice down.

Zoe Since then, everything's fallen apart. You're not allowed to go to school any more. I'm getting chased by half-crazed idiots, even my grandma won't answer the door to me. Am I such a terrible person, Tab?

Tab sits Zoe down.

Tab I'll say it again. This is not about you. It's nothing to do with what you said, it's nothing to do with you at all.

Zoe What is it then?

Tab It's better for all of us that it's kept a secret. Just know that I'll always be your friend. We all will.

Zoe You're not the only one with secrets, Tab. We're supposed to be friends. I'm not scared to tell you what's happened to me . . .

Tab Secrets are dangerous, Zoe.

Zoe I want you to . . .

Tab Keep it to yourself, whatever it is.

Zoe We're mates, it's important . . .

Tab No!

Zoe cries.

Zoe What's happening, Tab?

Tab I have to say goodbye.

Zoe I only just got here . . .

Tab I mean for ever. We're moving away, Zoe.

Zoe When?

Tab Can't . . .

Zoe (*angry*) . . . 'Can't say', how did I guess? (*Pause*) Sorry.

Tab Dad's had a place built in the country. Paradise he calls it. Anything but, if you ask me. It's in case . . . in case we ever had to move. Now we do.

Zoe I'm not leaving till you tell me what's going on, Tab.

Tab Go home, Zoe, please.

Zoe No.

Tab turns away.

. . . Give me the address, I'll come and visit.

Tab walks away from her.

. . . You will see me again, Tab. You will. I don't give up without a fight, you know.

Scene Sixteen

Thursday the 10th. Early evening. The Black Diamond Bar. Daz stands at the bar, knocking back a drink. He orders another, then heads for a seat. He bumps into Mick.

Mick   I thought you was more of a Blue Moon man.

Daz   Very funny. Don't think they'd have me in there in a hurry. Seen Cal lately?

Mick   Course, his right-hand man, aren't I?

Daz   Has he said owt? Not after me for last week, is he?

Mick   He scarpered after the trouble broke out. He dun't know you risked your neck to save the Subby tart and you've got me to thank for that, by the way.

Daz   They'd have killed her, Mick, and all her mates.

Mick   Whatever. You hear what happened to Wentworth?

Daz   Has he bought another Suburb or sommat?

Mick   Only in FAIR, i'n't he?

Daz   Wentworth? . . . You're joking, he's the biggest Subby there is.

Mick It's true, mate. The DS have got him, at least, they did have till Wentworth bought his way out of it. DS was gonna delete the whole lot of 'em I heard. Now they're getting exiled instead.

Daz How did he wangle that one?

Mick Bought themselves a bit of freedom. He won't get away from us that easy.

Daz Are DRED after him then?

Mick Daz, he's in FAIR and he's a Subby. What do you think? They're heading out on the old Highway, according to sources. That means they'll be coming through here. Correction, they'll be trying to.

Daz When?

Mick Tomorrow night. (*Pretending to shoot*) Mummy Wentworth, Daddy Wentworth and rich little baby Wentworth. (*Blows the end of his invisible gun*) Three more Subbies dead and a fair few peanuts gathered into the bargain. It'll be a synch.

Daz Are you gonna be there?

Mick Nah, mate. I just give the orders these days.

Scene Seventeen

Thursday the 10th. Early evening. The Askews' living room. Dawes is looking out of the window. Pohlman is leaning on the back of a chair. Gerald is escorting Amanda out of the room.

Amanda She's a little girl.

Gerald	Come along, darling, let the men do their work.
Dawes	We just want to talk to her, madam.
Amanda	She hasn't done anything.
Dawes	She's here.

Amanda and Gerald leave the room. Enter Zoe.

Pohlman	Hello, Zoe. I'm Lieutenant Pohlman, Domestic Security. This is Sergeant Dawes. We'd like to talk to you if that's all right?
Zoe	(*terrified and only just hiding it*) Sure.
Pohlman	Where have you been today?
Zoe	Didn't my parents tell you?
Pohlman	I'm asking you.
Zoe	Went to see a friend.
Pohlman	Name?
Zoe	Tabitha Wentworth.
Pohlman	Paul Wentworth's kid, right?
Zoe	That's right, yeah.
Pohlman	Did they let her see you?
Zoe	Sure.
Pohlman	You've had some trouble at school, I believe?
Zoe	What do you mean?
Pohlman	I think you know what I'm talking about. Mrs Moncrieff gave me a call. She had rather a lot to say about you, Zoe. I gather you have rather an unhealthy interest in brainwashing.
Zoe	There was a bit of hassle. It's over now.
Pohlman	(*leaning towards her*) Is it? (*Pause*) Don't some of the kids call you names? One name in particular.
Zoe	Can't think.
Pohlman	'Chippy lover' ring any bells for you?
Zoe	Some have. I don't take much notice.

Pohlman	Don't you like to have friends?
Zoe	They're not my friends.
Pohlman	Who are your friends, Zoe?
Zoe	I don't have too many right now. Maybe I don't have any at all.
Pohlman	You have at least one friend, don't you?
Zoe	Do I?
Pohlman	Sure you do. Just been to see her, haven't you?
Zoe	We've fallen out.
Pohlman	I'm surprised. I thought you had quite a lot in common.
Zoe	Tabby hasn't done anything . . .
Pohlman	Did I say she had, Dawes?
Dawes	No, lieutenant.
Pohlman	According to Mrs Moncrieff, you've been suggesting the State tells lies to people. Now you may be too young to realise this but when someone communicates an idea like that to others, it can cause a lot of damage. People become insecure, they begin to doubt, picking at newspaper articles for instance, questioning television bulletins. And of course we all know that if you're looking too hard for something, there's always a chance that you'll think you've found it. There was one news item, a couple of days ago now. Chippy lad on a murder-fest. One of the cameras caught a brief glimpse of a Subby girl. Running away she was. Someone who didn't know better could be fooled into thinking it was you.
Zoe	Have I done something illegal, lieutenant?
Pohlman	I don't know, have you?
Zoe	No.
Pohlman	A lot of good, respectable people pay their

Zoe	taxes to make sure you have a comfortable lifestyle. Would you want to lose all of this?
Zoe	No, lieutenant.
Pohlman	Then why make waves?
Zoe	It would be nice if 'all this' was available to everyone.
	Pohlman puts his face right up to Zoe's.
Pohlman	You'd better pray things stay as they are.

Scene Eighteen

Thursday the 10th. Early evening. Daz's house. Mrs Barraclough is coughing. Enter Daz. He's wrapping a bandage around his bruised torso. He's in a bad way.

Daz	You in the wars, our Mam?
	Pats her gently on the back.
	. . . There you go.
Mrs Barraclough	(*stops coughing*) What's with the bandage?
Daz	Got in a bit of a scrap, Mam. It's nothing to worry about.
Mrs Barraclough	I bet. Was it DRED, Del?
Daz	It's Daz, Mam.
Mrs Barraclough	Was it?
Daz	No.
Mrs Barraclough	Who then?
Daz	I fell off an elephant.
Mrs Barraclough	You're daft, lad.

Act Two, Scene Eighteen

Daz You don't know the half of it.

We hear a mobile phone ringing.

Mrs Barraclough What's that?

Daz Sommat to make me dafter.

Daz picks up the phone and takes it to a quiet corner. He's about to answer it, then stops quickly to put a jumper on. When he finally picks the thing up, it stops ringing. He sits with his head in his hands, Mrs Barraclough coughs once more. The phone rings again, he answers it straight away.

. . . Zoe, what's happening?

Zoe (*crying*) Daz.

Daz Are you crying?

Zoe Sorry, Daz. DS have been here. They were waiting for me when I got in yesterday. Dad's just had another go at me for it. He's hardly stopped since they left. I've never seen my dad so angry, Daz.

Daz Did he hit you, Zoe?

Zoe No, but having them here's about the worst thing you could do to him. He went ballistic . . .

Daz Don't cry, Zoe, please.

Zoe I've never felt so bad. If it wasn't for you . . . I don't know what I'd do . . .

Mrs Barraclough Who you talking at, Del?

Daz (*to Mrs Barraclough*) Me sen, Mam.

Zoe You there, Daz?

Daz Yeah. So what you gonna do?

Zoe Hope he cools down, I suppose. I'll just have to toe the line for a while. Daz?

Daz Yeah.

Zoe You do still like me, don't you?

Daz Course I do. So what were they after?

Zoe They mentioned the waste land thing, their version of it. They can't have any proof though . . .

Daz We'd be in a cell if they did.

Zoe I'd just been to see Tab. She's in some kind of trouble as well. It might have had something to do with that. I really miss you, Daz.

Pause.

. . . You still there?

Daz Yeah. I was thinking.

Zoe Everything's such a mess . . . You should hear him down there, anyone would think I'd murdered someone. What have I done that's so wrong? (*Pause*) Am I breaking up or something?

Daz No.

Zoe You seem quiet?

Daz I've got a lot on my mind.

Zoe You're not the only one.

Daz I've got to go, Zoe. I have to be somewhere.

Zoe Where?

Daz I can't say. There's something I've got to do.

The screen goes blank.

Zoe Daz, I . . .

Zoe realises Daz has hung up.

Scene Nineteen

It's Sunday the 13th. We hear the familiar 'clunk'. Gran appears in her beam of light.

Gran I'd give anything for just a glimpse of sunlight. It's strange the things you miss when you no longer have them. We don't realise we're doing it, but we spend half our lives in a daze. Worrying about things that don't really matter. You miss out when you do that. For such an advanced race, there's plenty of things wrong with us. Surely we're not meant to hate each other the way we do? We're timid little creatures when you think about it. Afraid of anything we don't understand. And instead of stopping to learn about these things, we just hate them instead. When I moved into my first house, I paid my next-door neighbours a visit. In twenty years, that was the only time they spoke to me and even then it was grudging. Why? Even to this day, I don't know. I'd never done anything to upset them. This sort of thing goes on all the time, it's happening practically everywhere you look. Neighbouring villages often don't get on. People at one end of a country don't like those at the other. Even today a lot of British people still moan about the French. Have you worked it out yet? They're all neighbours. They think they're frightened of each other but, really, they're not. They're frightened of themselves.

Scene Twenty

Evening of Friday the 11th. Inner City street. It's dark. Nel and Trev are patrolling, they each have a gun. Enter Daz. He spots them and ducks.

Nel First job then, Trev?

Trev First action.

Nel How do you like it so far?

Trev Nothing to it.

Daz throws a stone. Trev and Nel look to where it lands. Nel directs Trev with the point of her gun. Daz moves closer and hides once more. They just miss him.

. . . It'll be a rat or something. How are we doing for time?

Nel They should be through the border by now. Better keep our eyes peeled.

Trev Nel?

Nel Yeah?

Trev Is it true about Sampson?

Nel What have you heard?

Trev That's he's been uncovered?

Nel Someone squealed, yeah.

Trev Have we brought him in yet?

Nel No. It's a handover job. Cal wants the DS to take care of it.

Trev You'd think he'd want to do that himself.

Nel He thinks they'll make a better job of it, I suppose.

Trev I thought he hated Sampson?

Nel He hates what Sampson stood for. There's a difference.

Trev They'll delete him.

Nel What makes you so sure it's a man?

Daz shuffles, they turn.

. . . You hear something?

They shine their torches towards Daz. The beams just miss him.

Scene Twenty-one

Friday the 11th. Same time. Lights come up on Zoe's bedroom. Zoe is using her phone.

Zoe . . . I could hardly say who I really was, she'd never let you speak to me . . . I'm a Chippy lover, remember?

A spotlight fades up on Tim. He's at home, on the phone. He appears nervous.

Tim Are you all right?

Zoe I had to talk to someone. You're about the only person who hasn't turned on me. You don't mind me calling you like this, do you Tim?

Tim No. You can call me any time you like. What did you want to talk about?

Zoe I've . . . I've sort of fallen for someone.

Tim Go on?

Zoe It's someone you'd never expect? I can understand if you don't want anything to do with this, so don't feel you've got to . . . I want to ask you something.

Tim OK?

Zoe Is any of this making sense so far?

Tim Erm, I don't know. I never thought you'd turn to me, Zoe, not in a million years.

Zoe Why not?

Tim I'm not exactly one of the 'in' crowd, am I?

Zoe And I *am*, I suppose?

Tim What did you want to ask me?

Zoe Two things. I wondered firstly if it would be OK for us to see each other, just now and then?

Tim lets out a quiet yelp.

    . . . If I don't talk to someone soon, I think I'll go out of my mind. You don't have to say yes, I wouldn't want to cause any trouble for you . . .

Tim   It's no trouble, Zoe, honestly. Do you want me to come over?

Zoe   It's not a good idea right now, Tim, my dad's on the war path.

Tim   Soon then?

Zoe   Yeah. I really appreciate this.

Tim   You do? (*Beat*) What was the other thing?

Zoe   It's my grandma. She hasn't been answering the door, I'm worried about her. Do you mind calling round?

Tim   No. It's only over the road.

Zoe   Thanks, Tim. Look, I've got to go. I've got another call to make.

Tim   Is it all right if I ring you later?

Zoe   Sure.

Tim   Bye then.

Zoe   Bye, Tim.

Zoe ends the call. Tim dials another number.

Tim   . . . Hi, Ned? You're never going to believe this. I think Zoe's just asked me to go out with her . . .

Spot fades down on Tim. Zoe starts to dial another number.

Scene Twenty-two

Same time. Back to the Inner City street. A car engine is heard.

Nel This is it. Are you ready?

Trev As I'll ever be.

They pull balaclavas over their faces and take up positions on either side of the street. Trev stands very close to Daz, almost touching him, but he doesn't know he's there. Headlamps sweep across the stage.

Trev Is it them?

Nel Could be, wait till they're closer. Stay back.

Daz stands and creeps towards them. He takes a gun from his pocket. After a slight pause, Daz's phone rings out. He scrambles to find it and switch the thing off.

Nel (*shouts*) Behind yer, Trev!

Trev turns, Daz drops the phone and makes a dive for Trev's legs, knocking him to the ground. Nel fires a shot at Daz but misses. Trev gets to his feet, another shot is heard. Nel falls to the ground. Daz has just shot her. He's in shock.

Tab (*off*) What's happening?

Mr Wentworth (*off*) Stay in the car. Lock the doors.

Trev looks over to where the car is, then back at Daz.

Daz (*now aiming at Trev*) Start running.

Trev runs away. Enter Mr Wentworth with his arms in the air. Daz spins to face him.

Mr Wentworth Please. I'll give you anything you want, just let us through.

Daz	(*putting the gun away*) You must be Wentworth.
Mr Wentworth	That's right.
Daz	I'm Daz. A friend of a friend.
	Enter Tab.
Tab	You did this for us?
Mr Wentworth	Get back in the car, Tabitha. (*Taking his wallet out*) I really don't know how to thank you. Here . . .
Daz	Keep it. I did it for Zoe.
	Exit Daz. Lights begin to fade.
Mr Wentworth	Extraordinary.
	Tab spots the phone on the ground and recognises it as one of the pair she and Zoe had built. It's now broken. Tab and Mr Wentworth head back to their car. Mrs Wentworth enters briefly and puts her arms around Tab. Lights out.

ACT THREE

Scene One

Monday the 14th. Zoe's bedroom. Zoe is holding her phone. Tim is with her. Throughout the scene, Tim tries to hide his feelings for Zoe.

Tim . . . The one that carried your drinks from the bar?

Zoe That's him.

Tim But he's a Chippy?

Zoe That's what I've been trying to tell you. Who did you think it was?

Tim I don't know.

Zoe There's just something between us, I can't explain it. From the first minute we saw each other. Do you know what I mean?

Tim I think so. Are you sure he doesn't just want to . . . you know?

Zoe What?

Tim Well. He might just fancy you, have you thought about that?

Zoe Tim, you were there. You saw what happened. He risked his life getting us all out of there. (*On the phone*) It's just ringing out. (*Puts phone down*)

Tim Maybe his battery's dead?

Zoe I'll find out soon enough.

Tim It's a bad idea, Zoe.

Zoe It's something I've got to do. We're moving

away, Tim. In a couple of weeks' time, I'll be a hundred miles away. How's he going to feel then? I can't just abandon him.

Tim Have you talked to your grandma?

Zoe I can't, she isn't back yet.

Tim Where are you supposed to be moving to?

Zoe Dad's been offered a transfer. That's what he says. He's probably been begging for one ever since the DS came round. We're . . . they're moving to Sunnyford.

Tim What if he turns on you?

Zoe Who?

Tim The Chippy lad.

Zoe He won't.

Tim You don't even know him, though.

Zoe Tim, we love each other. I can't explain. I've just got to do this. I wouldn't stand in *your* way if you wanted to be with someone.

Tim I'm not standing in your way . . .

Zoe That's what it feels like.

Tim I'm worried about you, that's all. (*Pause*) Are you sure this is what you want?

Zoe I've never been more sure of anything. I know it sounds stupid, Tim, and I know what I'm letting myself in for, I do. You'll meet someone yourself one day, then you'll know what it feels like.

Tim I already do.

Zoe is stopped in her tracks. She looks at Tim in astonishment.

Zoe You . . .?

Tim nods.

. . . Who is it?

Tim A girl at school.

Zoe Why haven't you said anything?
Tim You never asked.
Zoe Is it serious?
Tim Depends what you mean by serious.
Zoe Do you love her?
Tim (*choked*) I think so.
Zoe Well, how would you feel if you could never see her again?
Tim Pretty bad.

Scene Two

Monday the 14th. Gran sits still in her chair. Lieutenant Pohlman is with her. The same sterile light shines down. We now see she is in a prison cell.

Gran We're all the same when it comes down to it.
Pohlman I doubt that.
Gran Some are more afraid than others.
Pohlman Getting scared, are we?
Gran I'm talking about you. Four days you've had me in this place. Has it done any good, do you think?
Pohlman Ask me in another four.
Gran Do you believe in your work, lieutenant?
Pohlman (*taking his hip flask out*) You could make this a lot easier for yourself.
Gran I doubt *that*.

Pohlman drinks from the flask.

	. . . Everyone has a conscience somewhere.
Pohlman	Is that the truth?
Gran	Yes, son. That stuff might help you ignore it for a while but it can't take it away.
Pohlman	You think you get to everyone, don't you? Manipulating your way in. Save your breath. You have no friends in this place.
	Exit Pohlman.
Gran	That's what he thinks.

Scene Three

Monday the 14th. Early evening. DRED HQ. Mick, Cal, Shaker and Trev. Shaker is standing over Nel's body.

Shaker	She was never gonna make it, Cal.
Cal	You were supposed to be there, Mick, I gave you an order.
Mick	I thought they could handle it, Cal. I wasn't to know she was gonna get wasted. They was only a bunch of Subbies. (*To Trev*) You must have seen something?
Trev	It was dark. The motor was drawing up, there was too much going on.
Mick	What did he look like?
Trev	Dunno. A young lad. Under six foot. I'd never seen him before.
Cal	Get out.
	Exit Trev.

Cal	Did she have any family?
Mick	No, Cal. DS got most of 'em when she was a kid.
	Cal makes to leave. Shaker takes a bullet from Nel's body and inspects it closely.
Shaker	I think you should take a look at this.
	Cal turns back. Shaker holds the bullet up to the light.
Mick	What's the problem?
Shaker	The pin mark. Different shooters leave different marks on the bullets . . .
Mick	So?
Shaker	You can tell what sort of gun someone's used by the mark it's left.
Cal	It's a start, I suppose. I want to know who did this.
Shaker	Work out who borrowed your shooter on Friday night, and you might have your culprit. (*To Cal, still holding the bullet*) This came out of your gun, mate.
	Cal stares into space. The others look concerned.
Cal	Barraclough.

Scene Four

Monday the 14th. Early evening. Silverdale, the border gate. Inner City dwellers are gathering at the gate. One male and one female guard organise the queue. Martha and Connie are up to their usual tricks. Zoe and Tim stand to one side. Zoe is wearing a maid's overall. Tim's holding a portable music system.

Martha   Tell you what though, Connie, I wouldn't be stuck out here unless I had to be, would you?

Connie   No.

Martha   I'd be in me fancy little house, guzzling chocolates and bringin' pleasure to me Subby husband. (*To Officer Linden*) You got an husband, love?

Officer Linden   Shut it.

Martha and Connie look at each other and then shake their heads.

Connie   Didn't think so.

Martha   (*to male guard*) What about you, handsome, you got a pretty lady stuffed away somewhere?

Officer Mian   No.

Connie   (*about Martha*) She's open to offers.

Connie and Martha have a good laugh. The action moves over to Zoe and Tim.

Zoe   Do I look convincing?

Tim   It fits you.

Zoe smears dirt on her face. Tim is wearing a money belt. It looks to be stuffed full of things. He takes it off and hands the thing to Zoe.

Tim   Put this on. I got a few things together. Things they can't get over there. You might be able to trade them. There's some cash as well.

Zoe   I don't want your money, Tim.

Tim   Take it.

Zoe   This is the nicest thing anyone's ever done for me.

Act Three, Scene Four

Tim You're worth it. (*Pause*) Ready?

Zoe As I'll ever be.

They head towards the gate, then split up. Zoe stands close to Connie and Martha. Tim puts the music system on the ground.

Martha . . . Connie, they don't know the meaning of the word. If you want a real one, you're better off on our side.

Connie Oh, no. I like to be 'tret' like a lady, me. Bit of romance, you know.

Martha Get you!

Connie Can't help being classy, can I? (*Beat*) Me sister's daughter's just got a gentleman.

Martha Has she now?

Connie Oh yes. Got a place of his own and everything.

Martha She should stick with 'im then.

Connie That's what *I* said. She's a sensible girl, mind you, won't rush in. They've been together nearly a month and they're not shacked up yet.

Martha (*sarcastic*) Classy.

Connie (*to Zoe*) What do you think, love?

Zoe What about?

Connie Do you like our fellas or Subby 'uns?

Zoe Ours.

Tim switches the music system on and starts to dance. His movements, and music, are sufficiently salacious to attract a crowd.

Officer Linden (*to Officer Mian*) What's that idiot playing at?

More people gather until Tim is completely surrounded.

Connie What's going on here then?

Martha Someone acting the goat. We'll never get home at this rate.

Zoe	I've seen him before.
Connie	Have you, love?
Zoe	Yeah. He turns up wherever there's people, and he . . .

Zoe whispers to Martha.

Martha	He doesn't?
Zoe	He does.

For a second, Martha looks shocked.

Martha	Come on, Connie!

Martha drags Connie into the crowd. Articles of clothing fly out from the centre of it. Zoe loiters around the few people that are still queuing for the gate. Tim's work is punctuated by cheers and applause.

Martha	Get 'em off! Get 'em off!
Connie	Put 'em on, put 'em on!

Raucous laughter.

Officer Mian	Shall I go and sort it?
Officer Linden	I think this is going to take two of us. (*To those still queuing*) Get your passes ready.

Those not watching the show get their passes out for inspection. There's a huge cheer from the crowd. The officers look concerned.

Officer Mian	(*to Linden*) Just let 'em through. We ought to get over there.
Officer Linden	Go on then. Single file.

The officers head over to the crowd, the others make their way through the gate. Zoe tags on the back of the queue and slips through.

Tim	Like what you see, missus?
Connie	Where are we looking?

More laughter. The officers push their way into the crowd. Tim makes a run for it.

Scene Five

Monday the 14th. Early evening. The Youthopia *theme tune plays. On the screen above, we see another excerpt from the programme.*

Nigel Welcome back. As you know, we've been keeping a very close eye on our two brave friends who, less than two weeks ago, met with a terrible fate in the name of peace and understanding.

Norma Our office has been inundated with messages of support from you, the viewers.

Nigel And Pippa spoke for the first time since their hideous ordeal this very afternoon. Felicity was there to capture the moment.

Cut to scene in a hospital. Pippa is wired to an unbelievable number of machines.

Pippa Where am I? What's happening?

Felicity You're in the Silverdale Medical Facility, Pippa. Do you remember what happened?

Pippa (*high drama*) I'm afraid. Can't . . . feel . . . body . . . Pain, violence. It's all coming back to me . . .

Cut to an expectant-looking Felicity.

. . . they attacked us, didn't they?

Felicity Yes, Pippa, I'm afraid they did.

Pippa Where's Edward?

Felicity I don't know quite how to tell you this . . .

Pippa He didn't make it, did he?

Felicity No.

Pippa It's all my fault . . . It was so stupid! I'm sorry, I'm so very . . .

Her machinery starts to flash and beep, doctors and nurses crowd around the bed.

Felicity A sad story indeed. But let's hope the life of this brave young man . . .

Doctor We've lost her . . .

Felicity . . . and woman, haven't been lost in vain. This is Felicity McColgan reporting from the Silverdale Medical Facility. Back to the studio.

Everyone suddenly relaxes. Felicity walks away from the camera, the doctors leave Pippa's bedside. Pippa then sits up and pulls the various tubes and wires away from her body.

Pippa Was I OK?

The other actors give her a round of applause.

Scene Six

Monday the 14th. Evening. Inner City street. A group of young Chippy kids are poking a dead body with a stick. One of them has a pair of big boots around his neck. Another's wearing a jacket that's far too big for her. Enter Zoe, she's lost and afraid.

Alf Hey missus, come see what we got.

Zoe pretends not to hear.

Sue Missus! He's got good doodies on him. They're still warm, an' all.

Kids laugh.

John You can have 'em cheap.

Act Three, Scene Six

Zoe goes over to them. They move out of their circle to reveal a body lying on the ground.

Alf Say what you're after, we get it off for yer.

Zoe This is a dead man. You should tell someone, not be fooling around with him, you could catch something.

Sue He's ours, missus. We found him first.

Alf After a pair o' nice boots? No holes or nothing.

Zoe How did he die?

John Who cares? What d'ya wanna pay for 'em?

Zoe Nothing. You should be ashamed of yourselves. Do your parents know you're doing this? I bet they'd be real pleased to know you're out here poking sticks at a corpse.

There's silence. Alf moves closer and looks Zoe over.

Alf You're a Subby, ain't ya?

Zoe (*wipes her nose on her sleeve*) Dressed like this, come on?

Sue Who'd you nick the trainers off? Only Chippy I've seen with a pair of them on their feet.

Kids start to crowd her, they become threatening.

John Maybe she's DS.

Zoe Listen, I'll be straight with you, OK? I was a Subby. I had to run away. I'm trying to find someone.

Alf Run away?

Sue Thrown out more like. 'Kick-out', are yer?

Zoe I'm here out of choice . . .

Alf No Subby comes here 'less they's forced to. You're a 'kick-out', missus, no mistake.

Zoe I'm looking for a man called Daz. Daz

Barraclough. Do any of you know him? He's suppose to live in the tallest tower block.

Sue Yer must have done sommat bad, eh missus? Kill some Subby, did yer?

Zoe (*taking money out*) Look. You think they'd let me keep all this if I had? Point me in the right direction and this is yours.

Kids glare at her for a second then snatch the money. They run away laughing.

. . . Come back!

Accepting defeat, Zoe looks around her. The sound of thunder rolls in, swiftly followed by rain. Zoe lifts her collar up and starts to walk. Lights fade.

Scene Seven

Monday the 14th. Night. Barraclough apartment. There's now a storm raging outside. Lightning occasionally flashes, illuminating the otherwise dark room. There's a hammering on the door. Enter Daz, half-asleep. He lights a primitive-looking lantern. The hammering continues.

Zoe (*off*) Is anyone in?

She continues to knock.

. . . Daz? Daz, it's me, Zoe.

Daz can't believe his ears, he scrambles to get the door open. Zoe runs into his arms.

. . . Daz!

Act Three, Scene Seven

Daz is motionless. Slowly, Zoe pulls away from him.

. . . Daz?

Daz I can't believe it. Look at you.

Zoe I had to get away.

Daz Did anyone see you?

Zoe Not too many.

Daz (*angry*) Are you stupid or something?

Zoe I'd never have found you, I only asked a couple of times.

Daz Asked?

Zoe I had to.

Daz Who?

Zoe Kids mainly. A gang about a mile or so away, then the ones hanging around downstairs . . .

Daz's anger visibly increases. He looks incensed.

. . . It's OK. They said they wouldn't tell anyone.

Daz I can't believe it.

Zoe (*upset*) I thought you'd be pleased. I thought you'd want to see me.

Daz I told you not to come.

Daz stares at her.

Zoe (*desperate*) Daz, I had to. We were moving away, I'd never see you again.

Daz (*shouts*) You'd never see me again anyway.

Zoe jumps at his words.

. . . Look what happened last time we saw each other? It's a miracle I made it home. How many bullets do you think I can dodge?

Zoe (*crying*) I thought we loved each other.

Daz It's not a fairy story. People like you don't get it together with people like me, it never works out . . .

Zoe But the phone calls. You said you missed me, you said . . .

Daz There's a difference. A bit of fun's one thing. This could get me deleted!

Zoe What do you think they'd do to me? This wasn't easy to do, you know. I've left everyone behind for you. Everything. (*Shouting*) All you can do is stand there and shout at me!

Daz (*grabs her shoulders*) I've wanted to see you more than anything else in the world. I've spent hours just thinking about it. Thinking about you. Wishing things could be different . . .

Zoe They can be.

Daz (*moves away*) They can't! (*Beat*) Look. Look where you are! Do you really think you could live here? 'Happy ever after' doesn't happen in places like this. This is all I am. All there is.

Zoe I don't care.

Daz Maybe I do. I don't want this for you. You weren't going to hear from me again. I was going to let you think I wasn't bothered. When you started talking about using the tunnel, all I could see were pictures of you getting hurt. I couldn't bear it. I couldn't bear the thought of you seeing me here, Zoe, and me having to watch someone as great and as beautiful as you stuck in a dump like this. I can't believe you're standing there. It's happening in front of my eyes. You've thrown your life away.

Zoe I'm starting a new one.

Daz I can't give you what you want . . .

Zoe I want this.

Act Three, Scene Seven 99

Daz (*shouts again*) No one wants this. How can anyone want this? There are dogs what live better than us.

Enter Mrs Barraclough. She's been woken up by the noise.

Mrs Barraclough What's going on?
Daz We've got a visitor.
Mrs Barraclough You trying to sneak lasses in?
Daz No.
Zoe We're friends.
Mrs Barraclough I bet. What's she got on?
Zoe It's a maid's uniform . . .
Mrs Barraclough I can see that. But what's a Subby doin' in it?
Zoe (*trying to lie*) I'm not a Subby.
Daz Leave it out, Zoe.
Mrs Barraclough Don't talk like a Chippy, that's a fact. Don't smell like one either. What you doin' here? Tryin' to get us both shot? (*To Daz*) Get rid!
Daz I can't, she's nowhere to go. I'll find somewhere for tomorrow. Let her stay for tonight. Please?
Zoe I haven't come empty-handed.

Zoe unfastens her overalls, revealing a bright red jumper underneath. She roots inside the money belt to see what Tim has provided for her.

. . . There's some soap, look. Erm, perfume! A cigarette lighter. It's gold, there's even some make-up.

Mrs Barraclough Fat lot o' good that'll be.
Daz She means well, Mam. We can't send her out on a night like this.
Mrs Barraclough Since when did you help Subbies?

Daz Since I fell in love with one.

Pause. Mrs Barraclough weighs up the situation.

. . . She needs us.

Mrs Barraclough Needs her head looking at. (*To Zoe*) No funny business.

Mrs Barraclough snatches the money belt then goes back to bed.

Daz She's not always like that . . .

Zoe I don't blame her. I'm sorry, Daz.

Daz opens his arms to her. Zoe cries, he strokes a tear away from her face.

Daz I didn't mean to get mad.

Zoe You *are* pleased to see me, then?

Daz Course I am. I just wish . . . I wish it could be nice for you. All the times I used to picture us together, I never once thought it'd be here. I had us in a massive house with a garden, driveway . . . you name it. I'm a builder like your mate's dad and you're the boss of a big bank somewhere. Every time you come home you make the place smell like flowers.

Zoe You had it all worked out then?

Daz I haven't told you about the kids yet.

Daz starts crying.

Zoe Daz.

Daz I can't look after you.

They hold each other as the lights go down. The storm appears to have waned.

Scene Eight

Monday the 14th. Prison cell. Gran is stretching again.

Gran Live life to the full. Know as many people as you can and take as many opportunities as are offered to you. Make mistakes by all means. It's better to have tried and got it wrong than never to have tried at all. Trust me, I've been around. It's Amanda that's the grand-daughter remember, not our Zoe. (*Sits down*) Zoe's mum was my son's daughter. Confusing, families, aren't they? My boy's dead now. They got him young, like his father before him. Gorgeous Gordon. I know. I should've told her. I didn't feel it was right at the time. Come on, I wasn't gonna spend a lifetime pining while I had his phone number, was I?

Scene Nine

Tuesday the 15th. Late afternoon. Chippy school. Daz, Zoe and Mr James.

Mr James Do you realise what you're asking me to do, Daz?

Daz You're the only one I could think of. Just for tonight, sir, please? If she stays at our place, the DS'll have her for definite.

Mr James And what about you?

Zoe Yeah, what about you, Daz? (*To Mr James*) Can't he stay here as well?

Daz I'll be all right. Please, sir. For all I know, they're round at our place now. There's been fans out all afternoon.

Mr James This is the girl they're looking for?

Daz Yeah.

Mr James (*he's heard the name before*) Askew? (*To Daz and Zoe*) Wait here. Don't leave this room, you hear me?

Zoe nods. Mr James leaves the room.

Zoe Do you think we should make a run for it?

Daz Stay here, like he said.

Zoe Daz, he's a Subby. He'll have gone to tell the authorities, we've got to get out of here.

Daz We stay.

Zoe Do you think they will be at your place?

Daz Course.

Zoe (*horror*) Daz! Oh no.

Daz What?

Zoe My jumper. Your mum said it was too nice so I took it off.

Daz So?

Zoe I left it on the floor!

Scene Ten

Tuesday the 15th. Late afternoon. Barraclough apartment. Mrs Barraclough sits motionless in

Act Three, Scene Ten 103

her chair. Lieutenant Pohlman is leaning over her, holding a bottle of pills. Officer Mian is searching the room.

Mrs Barraclough I don't have to say nowt to you. I won't either.

Pohlman About what, Mrs Barraclough? The young lady you've been harbouring?

Mrs Barraclough There's no one here.

Enter Sergeant Dawes.

Pohlman Anything?

Dawes Not yet, sir, the lads are still searching.

Pohlman We've been told otherwise, Mrs Barraclough. Are you sure you've nothing to tell us?

Mrs Barraclough remains silent.

. . . Dawes?

Dawes Sir?

Pohlman Get rid of these, would you.

Mrs Barraclough They're me medicine.

Pohlman Bit of a junky, are we?

Pohlman tips some of the pills into the palm of his hand. One by one, he drops them on the floor, crushing them with the heel of his boot.

. . . Once more with feeling, Mrs Barraclough. Where are they?

Mrs Barraclough Who?

Pohlman This doesn't have to get nasty. You could make it a whole lot easier for yourself.

Officer Mian *(to Dawes)* Place is clean, sarge.

Pohlman *(to Mian)* Check out the basement. *(To Mrs Barraclough)* That's where we found the other one.

Exit Dawes and Mian.

. . . Del, wasn't it. Now there was a helpful

	young man. Told us lots of interesting things, he did.
Mrs Barraclough	He were shot in street. Never told you owt.
Pohlman	We have some very clever doctors, Mrs Barraclough. He was in a bad way for quite some time, but we managed to keep him with us. He became quite the little chatterbox towards the end.
Mrs Barraclough	(*hiding her pain*) It's not gonna work. There's nowt for you here.
Pohlman	Don't get too comfortable. I may want to see you again.

Exit Pohlman. Mrs Barraclough cries briefly then pulls herself together. She takes Zoe's red jumper out from under her own.

Mrs Barraclough Can't see for looking, eh Del?

Scene Eleven

Thursday the 17th. Early evening. School hiding place. Zoe is half asleep. She's been in hiding for two days. A door opens in the floor, making Zoe jump. Mr James pokes his head through.

Mr James	Wake up.
Zoe	Are they here?
Mr James	I've brought you something to eat.
Zoe	I'm sorry to put you to all this trouble . . .
Mr James	Save your breath.
Zoe	Why are you doing this? You obviously can't

Act Three, Scene Eleven 105

	stand the sight of me. I didn't ask to be brought here, you know.
Mr James	I don't think you fully realise what's at stake. You ran away because you didn't want to move out of Silverdale . . .
Zoe	I ran away to be with Daz, I love him.
Mr James	And what Zoe wants, Zoe gets. You're a Subby all right.
Zoe	So are you. You don't have to be here either, you could be in a private school if you wanted. What are *you* doing here?
Mr James	Making a difference. Helping people who haven't had the opportunities you've had. So you think you're in love with Darren?
Zoe	I am.
Mr James	Is that worth risking his life? And what about his mother? These are people's lives you're playing around with. What about your own family? Have you stopped to consider how they must be feeling now?
Zoe	Let me out then, I'll take my chances . . .
	Mr James puts his hand over Zoe's mouth.
Mr James	The rest of your life is gonna be spent doing just that. I've got something for you. You've heard of FAIR, I presume?
Zoe	Daz said he thought you were involved . . .
Mr James	You're lucky to have such influential friends.
	Hands her a letter.
Zoe	What's this?
Mr James	The only chance you've got.
	Exit Mr James. Zoe opens it and starts to read.
Zoe	Grandma?

Scene Twelve

Thursday the 17th. Early evening. Barraclough apartment.

Daz Cal's got the place staked out, Mam, you've got to come with me.
Mrs Barraclough I'm stayin'.
Daz Mam, they're looking for us. They'll break their way in.
Mrs Barraclough Come here, son.
Daz kneels beside his mother.
. . . Go make a life for yoursen.
Daz No Mam . . .
Mrs Barraclough I handled DS. I'll do same for DRED. Do what yer can for that lass o' yours. Look after her, son.
Daz Come with me, Mam, there's room for two of us down there.
Mrs Barraclough I'm ready for a better place.
Daz But you can't . . .
Mrs Barraclough Me mind's made.
Daz I love you, Mam.
Mrs Barraclough Love you an' all, son.
Exit Daz.

Scene Thirteen

Still Thursday the 17th. School hiding place. Zoe is reading the letter.

Act Three, Scene Thirteen

Gran (*VO*) . . . Follow these directions once you get to the highway. They'll be waiting. I wish I could meet the boy. I hope he treats you with the respect you deserve. Chippy or no Chippy, he's bound to be better than the coward your mother married . . .

Lights up to reveal Gran writing the letter. (This is a flashback to the previous day.) Sergeant Dawes stands behind her.

. . . Your life won't be an easy one but I know you'll make it count for something. We're made of the same stuff you and me. Keep going, Zoe. Know that you have the power to make a difference and remember that you're never alone.

. . . Forever yours, Great Grandma. P.S. When you get there, remember to tell the Wentworths who sent you.

Gran puts the letter into its envelope and hands it to Dawes.

Gran Thank you. You'd better get going, son. It'll soon be time.

Dawes How can you be so calm?

Gran Would it help if I caused a scene, do you think?

Dawes I tried to stop it, you know that.

Gran I know.

Exit Dawes. We cross back over to Zoe in the school (back to Thursday 17th). Mr James is hammering on the trap door.

Mr James Open the door. It's me.

Zoe does as she's told. Mr James appears.

. . . The DS are here.

Zoe No!

Mr James If you leave now, I can get you out of the place.

Scene Fourteen

Thursday the 17th. Evening. Basement of Barraclough apartment building. Daz is hiding. A DS officer sweeps a torch around. We hear the muffled sound of helicopters. The officer speaks into a radio device.

Officer Adams   No sign of him in the basement. Over.

Officer Blake   (*VO radio*) Check the furnace, they hide in there sometimes? Over.

Officer Adams   Been there, boss. There's no one down here.

Officer Blake   (*VO radio*) Return to base.

Cal enters.

Cal   (*threateningly*) I'll take over from here.

Officer Adams spins around. Cal shoots him. Lights down.

Scene Fifteen

Thursday the 17th. Night. The Barraclough apartment. It's darker than usual. Mrs Barraclough is slouched in her chair. There is the noise of helicopters in the background.

Loudspeaker   (*from a helicopter*) . . . seen or heard anything, you will report to a Domestic Security officer. Failure to do so is an offence against the State.

The helicopter moves away. In the distance, we

can still hear the announcement being repeated. There is a gentle tap on the door. Mrs Barraclough doesn't react. A knock this time and the door swings open. Enter Zoe.

Zoe Mrs Barraclough? (*Creeps over to her*) It's Zoe. Can you tell me where Daz is, please? Mrs Barraclough?

Zoe places a hand on her shoulder. Mrs Barraclough slumps forward. She's been killed. Zoe stifles a scream then steps back.

. . . (*Telling herself*) Stay calm.

Mick appears from the shadows and grabs Zoe from behind. He puts his hand over her mouth.

Mick Good advice. No noise now. We're going for a walk.

Scene Sixteen

Thursday the 17th. Night. Basement. Daz is still hiding. Cal knows he's there. Cal has been joined by two other DRED members, who are holding torches.

Cal You can't stay in there for ever, Barraclough. You might as well get it over with. Brave little lad. Following in his big brother's footsteps. The trouble is, you're not as bright.

Daz (*off*) Still here, aren't I?

Cal For the minute.

Enter Mick with Zoe.

Mick Look what I found, Cal, it's the Subby tart.

Cal Hear that, Barraclough? You have a visitor.

Cal removes his glove and twists Zoe's ear. She cries out.

Daz (*off*) Zoe?

Cal You're keeping the young lady waiting. Where are your manners, lad?

Daz (*off*) Will you let her go?

Cal You have my word.

Zoe What are you going to do to him?

Cal Me? Nothing. Mick does the killing.

Zoe (*shouts*) Don't come out, Daz!

Mick (*to Zoe*) We'll kill you if he doesn't.

Cal Either way, Barraclough, we'll get you in the end.

Zoe What has he done? Is this because of me?

Cal Thinks a lot of herself this one. (*To Zoe*) Your bit of rough over there shot one of our members. He used the same gun that I'd given him to kill you with. (*Raised voice*) Isn't that right, Barraclough? (*To Zoe*) 'The only good Subby is a dead Subby', I believe were his words.

Zoe I don't believe it. Stay where you are, Daz.

Enter Daz, hands in the air.

Daz Let her go.

Cal All in good time, lad. Wouldn't want her fetching the law before we've finished now, would we?

Daz I'll be dead before she gets up the stairs.

Cal Are you in a hurry, Mick?

Mick No, Cal.

Cal This is a job we should take our time over. Nel, she was called. She lasted a few hours after you'd gunned her down. Only fair to do the

Act Three, Scene Sixteen

same for you. It's what she would have wanted.

Mick prepares his gun.

Zoe No!

Daz It's OK, Zoe.

Zoe (*desperate*) Daz . . .?

Mick Whereabouts, Cal?

Cal Knee. (*To Zoe*) This'll be a first for you, I suppose. You might want to cover your ears, there's going to be screaming. (*To the DRED members*) Hold him.

The two with torches hold Daz in position.

Zoe No, please.

Zoe tries to turn away but Cal keeps her head held towards Daz. Mick goes over to Daz, gun in hand.

Mick This is going to hurt.

Mick places the gun against Daz's knee and looks over to Cal.

Cal When you're ready.

Daz is breathing heavily. Zoe is shaking. A shot rings out. Mick and Daz are both jolted. Zoe screams. Slowly, Mick stumbles backwards, then falls to the floor. Enter Sergeant Dawes. The people holding Daz let go and reach for their own weapons. Dawes shoots them also. The torches are now on the floor. Daz runs to Cal and Zoe. Cal takes out a gun and holds it to Zoe's head.

Daz Take me out, Cal. That's what you came for. You gave me your word.

Cal aims the gun at Daz.

. . . I love you, Zoe. Don't forget me.

Zoe Never. I love you, Daz.

Another shot is fired. Zoe screams. Cal falls to the ground. (Dawes has shot him.)

Dawes The place is surrounded. If Pohlman sees you, there's nothing I'll be able to do.

Daz What's going on?

Dawes Get out of here.

Zoe Come on.

Daz and Zoe exit.

Scene Seventeen

Friday the 18th. Morning. Gran is wearing a grey boiler suit. She's being handcuffed by two DS officers.

Gran There are better jobs than this, you know. If you had worked a bit harder you might have had better prospects. Enjoy it, do you?

Officer Mian Shut it, lady.

Gran Lady. Very nice. Eighty years it's taken to find me. I wouldn't say that's much for you to be proud about. Do your mothers know you do this? You have got mothers, I presume? Maybe you killed them as well.

The officers escort Gran out of the cell. We hear the Youthopia *music as the programme appears on the screen.*

Norma . . . Welcome back to part seven of tonight's *Youthopia*. The only uncensored current affairs programme especially for the younger community. Nige?

Nigel That's right. Now, for the moment we've all been waiting for. Felicity, I believe you have a treat in store for us tonight?

Cut to Felicity holding a microphone.

Felicity Thanks, Nigel. I join you from outside the DS building. As you see, the streets are now deserted. Everyone having rushed home so as not to miss this historic event . . .

Norma (*VO*) Felicity.

Felicity Yes.

Norma (*VO*) Will Sampson be making an address, do we know?

Felicity I believe not, Norma. According to the press release, she has chosen to remain silent. We will see the actual event but in the interests of public taste and decency, cameras will only be permitted once the prisoner is ready . . .

Her voice and image fades out.

Scene Eighteen

Friday the 18th. Morning. The highway. Daz is asleep, Zoe is reading her letter. Her arm is bleeding and in a makeshift sling.

Zoe Daz?

Daz (*stirring*) Hmm?

Zoe We should get moving.

Daz sits up and rubs his eyes.

Daz (*looking at Zoe's arm*) How is it?

Zoe I've felt better.

Daz Try to keep it still.

Zoe Who'd have thought getting shot would hurt so much. Not like the films, is it?

Daz How long do you think it'll take us?

Zoe About three days according to this (*indicates the letter*).

Daz Do you reckon you'll be able to make it?

Zoe I'm not going to give up now. (*Reading*) 'Paradise'. (*To Daz*) I can't wait to see Tab's face. She told me about it once.

Daz About her dad being in FAIR?

Zoe (*surprised*) How do you . . .?

Daz Don't ask.

Zoe The past couple of weeks have felt like a lifetime. What do you think might have happened if I'd just gone home that day, if I hadn't been there when you came out of the tunnel?

Daz You were, though.

Zoe All this because of a stupid school play. If I'd have kept my mouth shut . . .

Daz Things happen for a reason.

Zoe That's what Gran said.

Daz It's hard to believe though, i'n't it? I always thought Sampson'd be . . .

Zoe A man?

Daz Yeah. She must be amazing.

Zoe She is.

Daz (*indicating the letter*) How did she get that to you?

Zoe The bloke who helped us escape last night.

Act Three, Scene Eighteen

Daz I don't get it.

Zoe Gran's one of his prisoners. He's a DS sergeant.

Daz That's hardly a reason to help her.

Zoe He's a member as well, like Mr James.

Daz She's got mates everywhere.

Zoe Do you think we're doing the right thing, Daz?

Daz Being together, you mean?

Zoe My parents probably think I'm dead by now. I asked Mr James if he'd get a note to them but he said they'd be better off thinking I was. And your mum, Daz.

Daz Most of her died when they got hold of Del. It wasn't you, Zoe, they just finished what had been started.

Zoe Everything feels so wrong.

Daz Not everything.

Zoe Do you think we are opposites, you and me?

Daz We're not so different really.

Zoe What was that other word you came out with?

Daz Which?

Zoe 'Diss' something.

Daz Dystopia.

Zoe Yeah.

Daz You pretended to know what it meant.

Zoe I wanted to impress you. So what is it?

Daz It's like someone's idea of a really bad place. Somewhere that's as bad as it gets. That's what Mr James said.

Zoe smiles.

Zoe So what's the opposite of that, do you think?

Daz This, maybe.

Daz kisses Zoe.

Zoe We've a long way to go.

Daz Better get started then.

Daz helps Zoe to her feet. They look at the letter, look around, then exit.

Scene Nineteen

Friday the 18th. Morning. Gran appears in spotlight. She is tied into what looks like an electric chair. Lieutenant Pohlman, Sergeant Dawes and several DS officers stand nearby. Officer Blake makes adjustments to the chair.

Gran You can take a person's dignity, deprive them of everything they've ever known, but one thing will always be there. You can't take a person's truth away. Something true will last forever. I'm afraid. I have a reason to be. I'd like to know what your reasons are. Fear feeds ignorance. Ignorance breeds injustice.

Pohlman Somebody shut her up.

Pohlman drinks from his flask.

Gran What do you hope to achieve . . .?

Officer Blake It's Operational, sir.

Pohlman Let them in, Blake.

Gran (*looking straight at Pohlman*) . . . A tyrant dies and their rule dies with them. A martyr dies and hers is just beginning.

Pohlman Clever words. It's a shame no one's listening.

Gran holds eye contact with Pohlman.

Gran Actions speak louder, lieutenant.

Gran takes a deep breath and looks straight ahead.

. . . Make it happen.

Pohlman signals Officer Blake to proceed. Blake places a gag over Gran's mouth. Members of the press enter. A camera is pointed at Gran. Her face appears in close-up on the screen above. Gran tightly closes her eyes. 'Clunk'. Blackout.

Before you Read

On pages viii–x, there is a list of characters with a brief description of each of them. You may find this useful until you get to know the characters during the course of the play. The questions that follow this section should also help you keep track of the story as it progresses.

Play-reading Tips

- If reading in a group, listen to everyone else. Don't just wait for your character to speak.
- Always read the stage directions. 'Actions speak louder than words!'
- Imagine yourself as the audience. This play was designed to be performed.
- Use all of your senses! Hearing is, perhaps, the most obvious but what about smells, tastes or even textures? Try to experience the world these characters inhabit.
- If reading on your own, try to create a 'mind cast'. Think of suitable actors for the various parts and imagine them performing the dialogue especially for you.
- Characters do not always say what they are feeling. Try applying the following questions: What are they saying? What do they mean? What do they want?
- Be aware of the playwright. Everything is there for a reason. Try to work out what those reasons are.
- Have faith. To get the best from a play, you should allow yourself to believe in the story. Use your imagination – let it take you right into what is happening.
- You may find it useful to prepare a selection of sound effects before you start. As well as using sound for specific things (gunfire, helicopters etc.), it can also be used to build atmosphere or suggest location.

Questions and Explorations

Keeping Track

Act One

Scene One
1. How old is Gran?
2. What are the 'two groups' called and what are they trying to achieve?
3. Who are the DS?
4. What does the line ' . . . *the few that are left have got a whole lot bigger recently*' (page 2) suggest to you?

Scene Two
1. Who is Sampson?
2. What has been sabotaged?
3. What were DRED planning to do with the shipment?
4. What impression of Cal do you get?

Scene Three
1. What does this scene tell you about the society these people are living in?
2. If the *Youthopia* programme were real, do you think you would enjoy watching it?
3. How would you describe the Askew household?
4. Which group would Gerald Askew be most likely to associate with: DRED, FAIR or the DS?
5. What impression of Zoe do you get in this scene?
6. How does Zoe feel?

Scene Four
1. What do you think the DS would do with Sampson if he was captured and handed over to them?
2. What is your impression of Cal now? How does this compare to Act One, Scene Two?

Scene Five
1. How does the relationship between Daz and his mother compare to that of Zoe and her parents in Act One, Scene Three?
2. Who was Del and what became of him?
3. Who is Roz? What do you think she is like?
4. Who would you prefer to be friends with, Daz or Mick? What are your reasons?
5. What was in the crates?
6. What does Daz think of Mick?

Scene Six
1. What does this scene tell you about Subby society?
2. What details in the scene suggest it takes place in the future?
3. What do you think of Larry?
4. What is the group planning, and why do you think they want to do this?
5. If there are two 'outsiders' in this scene, who would you say they are? (Do not include the *Youthopia* section.)
6. Which character do you identify with most?
7. What does Tim think of Zoe?
8. What are the '*communication codes*' (page 18)?
9. What opinion do Tab and Zoe have of Chippy boys?
10. What do you think happened to the Inner City family in the *Youthopia* section? What does this suggest about the DS?

Scene Seven
1. What do you think is the relationship between Zena and Lawson? What clues are given about it in this scene?

Scene Eight
1. Do you trust Mick? Give your reasons.
2. Is Roz what you expected? Can you imagine her and Daz together?
3. Who is Ned getting married to?
4. How does Tim see himself?
5. Who is the main troublemaker in the Subby group?
6. Why does Daz want to join DRED?
7. What sort of things do you think are going through Daz's head, before he throws the money into the air?

8   Who is the most cowardly person in this incident?
9   What aspects bring tension to this scene?

Scene Nine
1   Think back to Act One, Scene Six. What is ironical about Zoe's conversation with Tab in that scene, given her actions here?
2   How would you sum up Daz's behaviour in this scene and the previous one: brave, foolish, impulsive? Give evidence for your answer.
3   What do you think is going to happen in Act Two?

Act Two

Scene One
1 What events from Act One is Gran referring to here?

Scene Two
1 What does the school play tell you about the way Subbies view the Inner City people?
2 Do you think the school play is well written?
3 What does Zoe mean by '*propaganda*' (page 40)?
4 What other examples of propaganda have appeared so far?
5 Who plays the role of Sampson in this scene?

Scene Three
1 What do you learn about the IQB?
2 What does this scene tell you about Chippy society?
3 After reading the scene, what impression do you have of Mr James?
4 Who is the drawing of?

Scene Four
1 Gran talks about not having much time left. What might this suggest?
2 When were yellow roses last mentioned? Why might this be significant?
3 At the beginning of the 'flashback' sequence, what are Gran and Zoe discussing (page 44)?
4 Do you think Gran is typical of her generation? Give reasons for your answer.

Scene Five
1 How does the audience know what day it is?
2 What is Lawson's job?
3 What could Lawson mean by '*Might give the game away*' (page 48)?
4 Which guns are they talking about?
5 What could be the implications of Mick overhearing them?

Scene Six
1 Assuming Tab is at home, why would Mr Wentworth want to keep the girls apart?

2 Why do you think Zoe is being chased by gangs?

Scene Seven
1 Think back to Act Two, Scene Four. Gran says '. . . *leave it to fate*' (page 47). How might this line be relevant now?

Scene Eight
1 In which scene did Lieutenant Pohlman first appear?
2 Who do you think the tip-off is about? (See end of Act One, Scene Four.)

Scene Nine
1 What do you learn about the Wentworths from the conversation between Daz and Zoe?
2 After hearing about Del, what is your opinion of Daz wanting to join DRED?
3 In Act One, Scene Six, Tab and Zoe talk about communication codes. How would it affect the current scene if that conversation had not taken place?

Scene Ten
1 What relevance do Gran's words have to the kind of society she lives in?
2 Could this be relevant to the society you live in?

Scene Eleven
1 Who is Felicity's report about?
2 How truthful is the report?
3 How do you think Zoe feels in this scene, and what might be going through her mind?
4 What does Amanda think Zoe is crying about?

Scene Twelve
1 What do you think Cal needs to know?
2 Who informed Pohlman and Dawes about Lawson? (See Act Two, Scene Eight.)
3 Who do you think is the more brutal, Cal or Pohlman?

Scene Thirteen
1 Why can't Zoe use the tunnel?
2 How long have Daz and Zoe known each other?

Scene Fourteen
1 Which weapons are they talking about?
2 What does this scene tell you about Tab's father?
3 Before he is killed, how do you think Lawson feels? How does this compare to Zena's ordeal?
4 What does this scene suggest about Cal's methods and those of the DS?
5 Who would you say has the most integrity, Cal or Pohlman?
6 If the above question had been asked in Act One, would your answer have been the same?
7 Do you have any idea who Sampson might be?

Scene Fifteen
1 How did Zoe open the gate? (See Act Two, Scene Six.)
2 What reasons can you think of for the Wentworths having to move away?
3 What is the name of the place Mr Wentworth has built in the country?
4 Which other character has said, '*I don't give up without a fight*' (page 72)? What reaction might the audience have this time?

Scene Sixteen
1 What do you think of Mick now?
2 Does Daz trust Mick? Should Daz trust Mick?
3 Of which group is Mr Wentworth a member, and what difference does this fact make to how you understand the previous scene?

Scene Seventeen
1 What do you think went through Zoe's mind when she saw Pohlman and Dawes waiting for her?
2 If Zoe could speak freely, what do you think her response to Pohlman's speech would be?
3 Is Pohlman really interested in Zoe's safety? What is his real purpose in coming to see her?

4 What does this scene suggest about the freedom of Subbies?

Scene Eighteen
1 Why do you think Mrs Barraclough keeps forgetting Daz's name?
2 How does Daz's lack of attention make Zoe feel?
3 What is Daz about to do?

Scene Nineteen
1 What relationship does this speech have to the rest of the play?
2 Where is Gran?

Scene Twenty
1 In which scene did Nel and Trev last appear?
2 Who do you think Sampson might be?

Scene Twenty-one
1 How do you think Tim feels at the end of this scene?
2 Describe how Zoe thinks Tim feels at the end of this scene.
3 What effect will this have on the audience's emotions?

Scene Twenty-two
1 What brings tension to this scene?
2 Were any of your predictions about what would happen in Act Two correct?
3 What do you expect to happen in Act Three?
4 Do you have questions that you would like to be answered? If so, what are they?

Act Three

Scene One
1. Which evening are Tim and Zoe talking about?
2. What do you think Zoe is planning to do?
3. What are Tim's real reasons for trying to persuade Zoe not to cross the border?
4. What does Tim feel during this scene? What effect will this have on the audience?

Scene Two
1. Where is Gran?
2. Note the date. What was the date of her very first scene?
3. Who has the upper hand in this scene?

Scene Three
1. What incident led to Nel's death (page 83)?
2. How does Shaker know the bullet was fired from Cal's gun?
3. How does Cal know it was Daz that shot Nel? (Think back to the end of Act One.)

Scene Four
1. Why do you think Tim is helping Zoe?
2. What do Connie and Martha add to this scene?

Scene Five
1. What does this excerpt from *Youthopia* tell you about the earlier items?
2. How do you think the programme's viewers would react if they were to learn the extent of the presenters' deception?
3. Does this scene alter your perception of Subby society? If so, how?

Scene Six
1. How does the language used in this scene differ from other scenes? What does this help to achieve?
2. Does Zoe appear to fit in here?
3. When was Zoe told that Daz lived in the tallest tower block?
4. What does the thunder add to this scene?

Scene Seven
1 Were you expecting Daz to react the way he does when Zoe turns up? What is the effect of this?
2 How would you describe the atmosphere of this scene?
3 Why has the playwright included a storm? What effect does it have on the scene?
4 In one word, what is Daz feeling?
5 Both Tim and Daz were willing to make a sacrifice for Zoe. What are those sacrifices? Are there any similarities between them?
6 How do you think Tim would react if he had witnessed this scene?
7 At what point does Daz relent?
8 What are your feelings towards Daz at the end of this scene?

Scene Eight
1 How does this speech fit into the story?
2 Now you know where Gran is. Does it make you view her differently?

Scene Nine
1 When you last saw Daz and Mr James together, who were they talking about?
2 Why would Mrs Barraclough say Zoe's jumper was '*too nice*'?

Scene Ten
1 How has tension been created in this scene?
2 How do you think Pohlman knew where to look for Zoe?
3 This is the second time Pohlman has said '*This doesn't have to get nasty*' (page 103). Who did he say it to the first time?
4 What does he mean by '*clever doctors*' (page 104)?
5 Who do we have the most respect for at the end of this scene?

Scene Eleven
1 What is Mr James's opinion of Zoe? Do you share his opinion?
2 Do you think Zoe has made a mistake?
3 Why does Zoe say '*Grandma?*' as she reads the letter (page 105)?

Scene Twelve
1 What could be motivating Mrs Barraclough to stay in the apartment?

Scene Thirteen
1 What sort of expression would Zoe have as she reads this letter?
2 What does the letter suggest about Gran?
3 When Gran says *'We're made of the same stuff . . .'* (page 107), does it bring any previous moments to mind? If so, which ones?
4 Why do you think Dawes is helping? Did you expect this?

Scene Fourteen
1 Why do you think Officer Adams says the word 'basement'? How does this help the audience?

Scene Fifteen
1 How do you feel when Mrs Barraclough slumps forward?
2 Were you expecting Mick to be there?
3 Do you know where he is taking Zoe? If so, how were you told?

Scene Sixteen
1 How has tension been created in this scene?
2 Do you believe Cal when he says *'You have my word'* (page 110)?
3 When did Daz say *'The only good Subby is a dead Subby'* (page 110)? What does this reminder bring to the scene?
4 Do you think Daz would have died for Zoe?
5 Do you think Zoe would have died for Daz?
6 How does this scene leave you feeling? Give reasons for your answer.

Scene Seventeen
1 What feelings do you have about Gran?
2 How do you feel about the *Youthopia* team?
3 If this programme were on your TV at home, would you choose to watch it?
4 Who is Sampson? Did you already know this, and if so, what gave it away?

Scene Eighteen
1 When do you think Zoe was shot?
2 What do you think Zoe means by *'Not like the films . . .'* (page 114)?

3 Which scenes are brought to mind when Daz says, '*About her dad being in FAIR?*' (page 114)?
4 Do *you* think they are doing the right thing?
5 Is this a positive end to their story?
6 Is this a happy end to their story?

Scene Nineteen
1 At the beginning of Act Two, Scene Four, Gran says, '*Imagine you were going to be put on your own, maybe for the rest of your life. What would be the one thing you'd take with you?*' (page 44). What do you think *her* answer to this might be?
2 What does she mean by '*A martyr dies and hers is just beginning*' (page 116)?
3 Do you want Gran to die?
4 What sort of emotions does this scene evoke?

General
1 From which moment, would you say, does Zoe's story begin?
2 At which point is there no turning back for Zoe?
3 Look back to the questions for Act Two. You were asked who played the role of Sampson in the school play (Scene Two). What significance does it have?
4 Fate plays a large part in the events of this story. How much of what Daz and Zoe experience is actually within their control?
5 What changes have taken place in Zoe's character from earlier scenes in the play?
6 Has anything about Daz changed?
7 How does the play compare to Robert Swindells' original novel?

Explorations

A DRAMA/CHARACTERS

1 Casting Agents
- Collect pictures of people from newspapers and magazines and create an imaginary cast for *The Play of Daz 4 Zoe*. Try to match the faces to the characters.
- Choose a cast from people you know. You could even hold mock auditions.

2 Questionnaire
The character introductions at the beginning of this play are intended only as a guide. The actors portraying these characters must get to know them fully. Choose a character from the play and answer as many of the following questions as you can about him or her. Try to find clues in the text.
- What sort of place do they live in?
- Describe their home life.
- What is/was their best subject at school?
- How would they dress for a party?
- What is their best friend like?
- Are they unhappy about anything?
- Who is their favourite pin-up?
- What are they afraid of?
- What is their ambition?
- What do other people think of them?
- What are their hobbies?
- Do they like themselves?
- What is their favourite joke?
- What would it take to embarrass them?

3 Environment
- How someone decorates their house can tell us a lot about their personality. Choose a character from the play, then create a mental picture of that character's bedroom. Try to make this

as detailed as possible: imagine the floor, bed, posters, furniture, books, magazines, electrical devices etc. What can they see from their window? Do they live in a house at all?
- Invite someone into this imaginary room. You have two minutes to show your guest round. Describe the room to him or her.
- The guest then describes the room to the rest of the group.
- The group tries to guess the chosen character.

4 Role Play
- Each member of the group selects one of the characters. (It is all right if more than one person chooses the same character.) Each person takes a few moments to think about their character – how they speak, move, laugh and so on.
- Everyone takes it in turns to sit in front of the rest of the group, in character, trying to answer any questions about their character that the group can think of. If the questions are too difficult, and only then, they can say, 'None of your business' and move on to the next question.
- Discuss what the group has discovered about the characters. Were the answers in keeping with the text?

5 Rules for Improvisation
In the following section, there are several scenarios to explore through improvisation. Discuss the term 'improvisation', making sure everyone knows what it means in the context of drama.
- When improvising scenes, the following mistakes often occur:
  a) Backs to the audience.
  b) Actors talking over one another.
  c) Voices too quiet.
  d) Giggling.
  e) Stonewalling.

Stonewalling means that actors are not co-operating with each other, e.g.
    Actor 1 I've just been to the shops . . .
    Actor 2 No you haven't, they're all closed.

Encourage members of the group to accept what their fellow

actors are giving them and then to build upon it, e.g.
> **Actor 1** I've just been to the shops . . .
> **Actor 2** Great! Did you buy me a present?

- The rules of improvisation are that you mustn't make any of these mistakes. Try playing the following rule game.
- Divide the group into smaller teams, giving two or so of the rules to each one. They then have to improvise a short scene in which these rules are broken.
- The audience should shout 'Stop!' whenever they see a rule being broken, and offer a correction.

6 Improvisation Scenarios

Del and Daz

In *The Play of Daz 4 Zoe*, we learn many things about Daz's older brother Del, but he does not actually appear. Create a scene in which Del talks to Daz about being a member of DRED. Include information about the tunnel (See Act Two, Scene Seven).

The Blue Moon Club

In Act One, Scene Eight, the following stage direction appears: *'There's a loud crash and then a scream.'* (page 33). The excerpt below shows us how the trouble starts, but the rest is left to the imagination. Create a version of what happened, starting from the lines shown here. End your scene on the scream.

> **Larry** Chill out, Chippy.
> **Jim** I wanna know what yer said.
> **Larry** Hard to explain, mate. I was talking in English.
>
> *Jim looks angry. Larry attempts even fancier dance moves. People in the club are gathering around to watch.*

This improvisation could benefit from a little planning. It might also help to follow these suggestions:
- Avoid a complicated fight sequence.
- Use all the characters present in the club.
- Remember most of them have been drinking.
- Create more speaking characters if it makes the scene easier.
- Try to keep your improvisation in context with the rest of the play.

Justice
Lieutenant Pohlman stands before a court of human justice. He is accused of committing crimes against humanity. Using only incidents and characters that appear in *The Play of Daz 4 Zoe* as evidence, create a courtroom drama.

Things you will need:
- a Defence team
- a Prosecution team
- evidence
- time to prepare the cases
- witnesses
- a judge.

Once you have done this, you could put other characters from the play on trial and see how they compare.

7 The Rule Game

Sit the group in a circle. Someone is sent out of the room while the group invents a rule. When the person returns, they put questions to individual group members. From the answers given, they must then try and guess what the rule is. They are not allowed to ask directly what it is! Once the rule has been guessed correctly, the last person who was asked a question leaves the room while the group thinks of another rule.

Examples of rules:
- Touching a part of the body after answering.
- Saying 'erm' each time you answer.
- Looking at the ceiling while you answer.

Once you have got the hang of it, try making the rules more complicated.

8 Resolution

For this activity, the group needs to be split into three. One group of people (the Journey Makers) are trying to get from one place to another. In order to do this, they must pass through unfamiliar territory. Part of this territory is governed by a tribe who call themselves the Miners. The following rules apply to each group.

Group 1. The Journey Makers
- You are essentially peaceful but must get to your destination at all costs.
- Create a reason for your journey.
- All you know about the Miners is that they mine a precious mineral from which most of your people's wealth is derived.

Group 2. The Miners
- You expect anyone visiting your land to abide by your rules. If they do not, they are imprisoned and forced to work in your mines.
- You will need to create these rules. Bear in mind that workers often die in your mines and you are always eager to take new prisoners.
- The Negotiators buy your mineral at a very low rate even though their people make large profits from it.
- You will need to create your territory.

Group 3. The Negotiators
- You have diplomatic immunity. The Miners' rules do not apply to you.
- Your task is both to secure more of the mineral and to persuade the Miners to free any imprisoned Journey Makers.
- You can afford to pay more for the mineral but do not want to.
- One of the Journey Makers is injured and will die within the day if they are forced to remain.
- You will need to know where the Journey Makers are heading and why.

Once your groups have assimilated the information above, begin the activity as follows:
- the Journey Makers make their way through the Miners' territory
- rules are broken
- prisoners are taken
- prisoners are set to work in the mines
- one person is badly injured
- enter the Negotiators.

Allow reasonable time for the scenario to run its course, then discuss the events with the other members of the three groups. What did you find? Try answering the following questions:
- Could a mutually acceptable resolution be found?
- Which party was the most willing to compromise?
- Which party should have been the most willing to compromise?
- What comparisons, if any, can you draw between this example and issues raised by the story of *Daz 4 Zoe*?

B WRITING

1 What is Drama?

Drama is about conflict. It can occur in many different ways but it has to be there. Without conflict, there is no drama. If the characters in this, or indeed any other, play were not given problems to face, there would not be much worth watching. The same goes for other forms of writing. Have you ever watched a film, for example, in which all of the characters are happy throughout? Characters need to be given problems. By their reactions to these problems, we have a source of conflict. Conflict is what engages an audience. Conflict creates drama.

> **CHARACTER + PROBLEM × REACTION = DRAMA**

The above rule can be applied to all forms of writing. It can also be applied to parts of a work, or to the work as a whole. Here is an example of how the rule can apply. In this instance, it is only a small part of the entire scene:

End of Act Three, Scene Three (page 89)

Nel has died. Shaker has been able to identify the murder weapon by inspecting the bullet.

Shaker   Work out who borrowed your shooter on Friday night, and you might have your culprit. (*To Cal, still holding the bullet*) This came out of your gun, mate.

Cal stares into space. The others look concerned.

Cal   Barraclough.

a) Our attention is drawn to Cal. **Character**
b) Nel has died. Cal's gun was used to kill her. **Problem**
c) Cal is angry. **Reaction**
d) The audience is engaged. **Drama**

In this example, not only is there **conflict** between Cal and the culprit (Daz in this case) but, if we look deeper, we also find 'inner conflict'. Cal gave the gun to Daz in the first place; this action might have been the cause of Nel's death. This example shows that conflict can occur between a character and their own conscience, as well as with other characters around them.

Look at the character of Gran, for instance. She is alone most of the time but still manages to hold our attention. She also provides examples of inner conflict. Go through her speech at the beginning of Act Two, Scene Four and see if you can find examples.

2 Dramatic Irony

There can be exceptions to the conflict rule. Sometimes, characters are given problems but they do not react. Look at the end of Act Two, Scene Five, where Mick has been eavesdropping on Zena and Lawson's conversation. The implications of what he hears are huge but neither Zena or Lawson react. This is because they are not aware of the problem. In these situations, the drama is created by the audience: *they* do the reacting. This type of conflict is known as **dramatic irony**. In the example above, the audience can see Zena and Lawson's predicament and they also see what could happen – but the couple themselves have no idea.

Dramatic irony can empower an audience by making them feel wiser than the characters they are watching. However, it can also evoke feelings of helplessness.

- Did you feel empowered or helpless while you were reading *The Play of Daz 4 Zoe*? Identify the scene(s) where you felt that way and try to explain why.
- Look for more examples of dramatic irony in *The Play of Daz 4 Zoe*. Start with the scenes between Tim and Zoe.

Questions and Explorations 137

3 Looking for Trouble
See if you can find the **conflict rule** at work in the following examples:
- Act One, Scene Two
- Act Two, Scene Seven
- Act Three, Scene Nine
- a recent episode of a soap opera
- your favourite film
- a fairy story
- a nursery rhyme.

4 Causing Trouble
- Write your own scene of **conflict** and then ask the group to act it out for you. Was it effective? How might it be improved?
- Rewrite your scene, introducing a moment of **dramatic irony**.

5 Love Stories
Romeo and Juliet
At the heart of both *The Play of Daz 4 Zoe* and the original novel, there lies a classic love story. Perhaps the most famous of these is the story of Romeo and Juliet. From what you know of *Romeo and Juliet*, see if you can pair together any of the people from the following two lists. In each case, discuss the main differences.

1 The Chippies	☐☐	a) The Nurse
2 Daz	☐☐	b) The Capulet family
3 Zoe	☐☐	c) Romeo Montague
4 Mr James	☐☐	d) The Montague family
5 Gran	☐☐	e) Friar Lawrence
6 The Subbies	☐☐	f) Juliet Capulet

Your Version
Most love stories contain the following points:
- a boy meets a girl
- they fall in love
- they are forced apart
- they are reunited
- there is a price to pay.

Draw up a list of other love stories and see if you can find any other common occurrences.

Write your own love story using the following points as a guide:
- Introduce the characters and show us a little of their everyday life.
- Introduce the notion of love.
- Show an aspect of loneliness.
- Show your characters getting closer together.
- Create a situation where they miss each other.
- Bring them together by chance.
- They make a date and go home happy.
- *A* has to go away to fulfil an unforeseen commitment. He/she has no way of contacting *B*. At this point, each one knows they are in love.
- *B* turns up for the date. How long does he/she wait before giving up?
- *A* thinks it is all over.
- *B* tracks down *A*.
- They run away together. *A* has to abandon the commitment.
- End by showing how the characters have changed. For example, you might have told us early in the story that *A* is terrified of flying but in order to find *B*, a long plane journey was necessary.
- Suggest their problems are not over.

TIP: Know how your story will end before you start to write it.

6 Letters
- Write a letter to someone in your class, as though it were from one of the characters in the play. Explain your most serious problem. Let the recipient know exactly how you feel. End the letter by asking for their advice.
- Reply to someone else's letter.

7 Gran's Story
Throughout the play, we learn quite a lot about Gran, but many of her actions and experiences are left to our imagination. Go through the text making appropriate notes and then write her life

history. Start by describing something that happened in the year she was born.

8 Public Executioner
In Act One, Scene Three, the following lines appear as part of the *Youthopia* programme:

> **Norma** Join us after the break for another of our popular Career profiles . . .
>
> **Nigel** Is being a Community Executioner as respectable as they try to tell us?

Later on, we are told that this 'profile' has been responsible for jamming the studio's switchboard. Write a script for this section of the programme. The object is to make the piece as believable as you can, while, at the same time, peddling lies and propaganda. Was the switchboard really jammed?

C PRODUCTION

Although reading plays can be enjoyable, the real purpose of the play script is to act as a blueprint for a live performance. In this next section, we will be looking at what would be needed to put *The Play of Daz 4 Zoe* on stage. Energy and commitment will be required to achieve such a goal, not to mention an ability to work as part of a team. The workforce needs to be divided into the following groups:
- set design
- wardrobe
- props
- lighting and sound
- special effects
- video.

1 Set Design
Imagine you are a professional design team. Your producer has given you a copy of *The Play of Daz 4 Zoe* and asked you to design the entire set. You have a very low budget and so huge, West End-style sets are out of the question.

Things to consider
When watching a play, there is nothing worse than long, laborious scene changes. You need to come up with ideas for things that would be quick to get on and off the stage. Remember that scenery can take up a lot of space. Will there be sufficient room to store your scenery before and after it is brought on to the stage? You might also consider a promenade performance; this is where you take the audience to the location, rather than putting the location in front of the audience.

Things to do
- Find out how many different locations are used in the play, then make a note of how many times each location appears. It might be useful to draw up a separate list for each act of the play.
- Find out how long you will have to make the necessary scene changes. (In many cases, the script will have allowed for this. Look at the stage directions.)
- Draw sketches of how you would like your sets to look.
- Draw a plan of your stage (have one copy for each of the locations). Now draw your sets on to these plans.
- Ask the Video team if they need sets or backdrops for their recorded sequences.
- Ask the Lighting and Sound team for their suggestions.
- Prepare a presentation of your set design plans for the other teams. Be sure to give credit for the advice you were given.

Suggestions
- When you have to establish a large number of locations, it is often best to choose an object or piece of furniture that best *suggests* that location. Also, do not underestimate the power of sound and lighting.
- Once you have identified which locations are used most often, you could arrange for these to be permanent fixtures on the stage. If not permanent, they can remain for the whole of that act.
- Divide your stage into sections. (With scaffolding, you could even create an upper level, which would be ideal for the more permanent locations.) While the action takes place in one section, the set could be being changed in the other(s).

- Write instructions for the play's technical crew. Tell them which sets should be changed and when.
- If you have a room big enough, you could place the audience in the middle and build the sets around where they will sit. You could even stage an open-air production, and get your audience to take a short walk from one set to another.

2 Wardrobe

It is your job to decide what all the characters in *The Play of Daz 4 Zoe* will wear. You will also be required to oversee everyday character make-up and hair styling.

Things to consider

There are several non-speaking roles in the play. You need to identify these. Also, several types of uniform appear in this play. Maybe you could borrow these from somewhere. Do not forget the video sequences. You should also be aware of how long your actors have between scenes to get in and out of their costumes. Look to see how the playwright has tried to make this easier.

Things to do
- Make a list of all the main characters.
- Make a list of the non-speaking characters.
- Look for clues in the script and cast list as to what they may be wearing.
- Liaise with the Special Effects team. (They are responsible for special make-up requirements.)
- Sketch your designs.
- Prepare a presentation for the other teams. Remember to give credit to those who have helped you.

Suggestions
- The costumes may need to be washed after every performance.
- In the Cameron Mackintosh production of *Les Misérables*, the entire stage crew wore period costume. In this way, they could walk on stage when necessary, without causing a distraction. Ask the Set Design team if this idea might help with their plans

for this production. Perhaps one of your uniform designs would be suitable?

3 Props

The term 'props' is short for properties and it refers to all the things, except sets and costumes, that your actors will need to perform the play.

Things to consider

Take note of everything: nothing is insignificant. The gun in Act One, Scene Two, is just as important as the flowers appearing in Act Two, Scene Four. Something else to bear in mind is the futuristic element. At the end of Act One, Scene Eight, Daz throws some cash into the air. We can assume they are banknotes, but would they look the same as the ones we have today?

Things to do
- Fill out the following chart:

SCENE	CHARACTER	PROP

- Make a props list for each of the actors.
- Check your lists against those of the Special Effects team.
- Find out which props can be obtained ready-made, and where from.
- Make a list of the props that need to be made.
- Work out how the props are to be made, listing the materials required.
- Prepare a presentation for the other teams. Credit those from other teams who have helped.

4 Lighting and Sound

You are the creators of atmosphere. Your job requires technical skill and a creative mind. You will be working very closely with the Video and Special Effects teams so it might be helpful to appoint a go-between.

Lighting
Things to do
- Make a list of the lighting directions in the text.
- List all other lighting requirements.
- Describe the mood you want to create for each scene or location.
- Bear in mind the time of day at which the scene takes place.
- Discuss the mood created by different colours.
- Prepare a presentation of your ideas.

Suggestions
- The most important things on a stage are the actors. If your lighting effects are more noticeable than them, then you have tried too hard.
- Where there is light, there are also shadows. These can sometimes be useful but can often make the stage look messy. Make sure the Set Design team are aware of this problem.
- There are two main ways to use light. One is a WASH, to light a large area. The other is a SPOT, to pick something out. You can use both at the same time and use colours with either – but remember the first point.

Sound
Things to do
- Make a list of the sound effects that appear in the stage directions.
- Make a list of suitable background noises.
- Work out how to create the sounds. Should they be performed live or pre-recorded?
- Note how long the various sounds need to run and how many times they are used.
- Ask the Set Design team if they need extra time with any of their changes.
- Prepare a short presentation.

Suggestions
- Sounds are there to bring a scene alive, not the other way around!

- Make a list of songs or pieces of music that evoke similar emotions to certain scenes in the play.
- What effect might it have if you played a love song after Zena and Lawson's interrogation scene?

5 Special Effects

It is your team's job to come up with simple, yet effective, ways of making the more unusual things in *The Play of Daz 4 Zoe* come to life. Your producer has asked for ideas that won't cost too much money but will still be convincing to an audience. You will also be responsible for special make-up requirements.

Things to consider

Remember, the simpler the better. Make sure your ideas are safe for the actors. Check with your Set Design team, so that you don't end up working on the same things.

Things to do
- Make a list of all the special effects needed.
- Ask the Video team if they need anything.
- Suggest a few ideas to the rest of the team and then try to simplify them.
- Draw diagrams to illustrate how your ideas will work on stage.
- Work closely with the Lighting and Sound team; you may need each other's help.
- Prepare a presentation for the other teams.

Suggestions
- Do not get too carried away with blood and gore.
- Remember, your effects may have to be repeated night after night.
- Fake blood can permanently stain fabric. Check this out with your Wardrobe team.

6 Video

You are responsible for all of the video sequences.

Things to consider

Filming can be a long and arduous process. You must plan for everything. You may need to find suitable locations and must ask permission before you can use them. Equipment is also important. What sort of camera will you use? Do you have access to an editing suite? You will need to work very closely with your Lighting and Sound team.

Things to do
- Make a list of all the video sections in *The Play of Daz 4 Zoe*.
- Draw storyboards for each section. (A storyboard is like a comic strip drawing.) Consider how the finished film will look.
- Do these sections need sounds or music?
- Will you require sets or backdrops?
- Are any special effects required?
- There may be scene changes happening on stage while your video sequences are being shown. Your Set Design team may need to know how long your sections will run for.
- Prepare a short presentation describing your ideas.

7 Presentations
Each team now makes their presentation to the whole group, allowing time at the end of each one for questions and answers.

8 Role Allocation
Many of the 52 speaking parts, especially the smaller ones, could be played by other members of the cast. Identify which roles could be played by the same actor, paying particular attention to the time needed for any costume changes.

9 Temporal Markers
In many of the scenes in *The Play of Daz 4 Zoe*, 'markers' have been deliberately included in the script to enable the audience to keep track of time. However, some directors may feel it necessary to convey to the audience the day and date information included in the directions at the start of a scene. How could this best be done?

D OTHER ACTIVITIES

1 *Youthopia*
The producers of *Youthopia* have decided to create a newsletter for their viewers. It is your job to write the first issue. Your brief is as follows:
- Make sure the style is in keeping with the programme.
- Include a 'Norma's Fashion Tips' feature.
- Include a 'Nigel's Fact File'.
- Let the readers know what is coming up in the following weeks' shows.

2 Oppression
In Act Two, Scene Three, Mr James asks his class to prepare a discussion about social oppression. Using examples from world history or from well-known fiction, prepare a five-minute presentation on this theme.

3 Radio Play
Suppose you are a radio producer hoping to broadcast *The Play of Daz 4 Zoe*. You must first go through this script looking for things that, in their current state, would not work on the radio. Once you have done this, draw up a list of changes to be made.

4 Photostory
Retell a section of the story of Daz 4 Zoe using photographs, captions and speech bubbles. You will need a camera, some actors, relevant costumes and some preparation time.

5 Name that Scene
Read some random lines from *The Play of Daz 4 Zoe* to the rest of the group. Points should be awarded to anyone who can spot the following:
- the character speaking
- the next line
- the Act in which it appears
- any accurate information about the rest of the scene.

Daz 4 Zoe

Torch

~~Binbag~~

Cover book

Remote control - Sky tv

Drink - screw top refill

Partaay - Monday

Contents, with all units, reading log

title, author, date, genre, mark out of ten.

acessories - hula outfit
food, drink, shoes ?